A SOUL FOR SALE

a true story

Carol Kornacki

A Soul for Sale
A true story by Carol Kornacki

Published by A&A Books
www.carolkornacki.org

Cover design by Archer Graphics

Library of Congress Control Number: 2010901979
International Standard Book Number: 978-0-9844370-0-9

First Edition
Printed in the United States of America

This book is dedicated to Aaron and Abigail.

My precious ones, you have decorated my life. Words cannot sufficiently express the love that I carry in my heart for you. You have loved me unconditionally and brought me unspeakable joy. My prayer is that when you have read this book, you will understand that all the pain and agony I've suffered through the years came to an end the day I met the Lord and then held each of you in my arms.

And…

Lorraine Araquistain

This book would be incomplete without a special thanks to you. How many times you said these words: "Carol, your life story needs to be told; it gives hope to a hopeless heart." Lorraine, you have spent the whole of your Christian life investing in souls. Whatever it required, you made the sacrifice! I believe this book is part of your work! Great is your reward.

Acknowledgments

Marilynn Kornacki Bonner
   I love you baby.

Linda Smith
   This story might not have ended as it did, had you not answered the call to rescue me. From the bottom of my heart, I thank you for loving me when I was unlovable, for reaching out to me when everyone else had given me up for dead, and for leading me to the only "One" who could give my life back to me.

Joe and Gwen Frey
   God spoke to your hearts to get this book out and you ran with it. A million thanks! You are genuine and that is rare. Thank you for being my friends.

Jackie Golba
   "A friend loves at ALL times" —that is you, Jackie.

Susie Kokanovich
   There is so much to thank you for—the countless hours you spent reading and rereading this manuscript, and your keen eye for the cover design. But, above all, I am grateful for your prayers!

Priscilla Blanks
   Your work on this book has been a big undertaking. I see your fingerprints throughout it. Thank you for your tireless work and dedication to "getting it right."

   A very special thanks to **Phil Blanks**, your friendship is priceless!

Contents

Introduction

The pages you are soon to turn will lead you through a storied past. All of the people you have known and the stories you have heard may well pale in comparison. This is the story of an often frightening, always tragic, life full of chaos and surreal circumstances. This is the tale of a compromised spirit, a searching soul and a broken woman. Turn the next pages and you will be committed to a journey that rivals any I have known or heard of! Easy to read and sometimes hard to digest, there is a powerful message contained within; I have never been the same since hearing it, I don't think you will be either.

Christi Cross Fenton

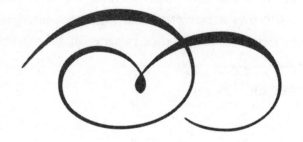

CHAPTER ONE

A Dead Girl Walking

The Arrival

We drove through the city streets without speaking. Every now and then, I could hear Richard sighing. He had agreed to come with me, but I suspected he was having second thoughts.

When we arrived, the parking lot was packed. After circling the building at least three times, he spotted an open space and raced over to get it, cutting off a person who was about to pull in. He shut off the ignition and we sat there staring out the window. Then he said, "Carol, before we go in here, can I ask you a question?"

I avoided looking at him. "Sure, go ahead."

"For the last six years, you have been practicing witchcraft. You do incantations, cast spells, read cards and communicate with the dead. Don't you think that this is a bit out of your league?"

I was annoyed at his question. "Yes, in fact, it is way out of my league, Richard. However, I'm curious. You agreed to do this. You're not backing out now, are you?"

He shook his head. "No, I'm not, but I think coming here is a waste of your time."

"That's a laugh. According to the doctor, I'll be dead soon. So tell me, my husband, does it really matter how or where I spend my time?"

Rather than answer my question, he reached under the seat and pulled out a bag. "Before we go in here, I'm getting high."

I snickered, "We've been on a perpetual high every day for the last ten years!" In spite of my sarcasm, I wanted a hit as badly as he did, if not more.

He opened the plastic bag, stuffed some of the contents into a pipe, struck a match and drew the smoke deep into his lungs. Then he passed it to me and I did the same. The stuff went right to my head. I let out a soft sigh and sunk down into the seat. Complete silence.

A few minutes later, he sat up, put his stash back under the seat, opened the car door and announced, "I'm ready; let's go."

"Wait a minute," I protested, "give me a second. I need to pull myself together."

He slammed the door shut, pulled a cigarette out of his pocket and fired it up.

A Killer Virus

I flipped down the visor and gazed at my ragged reflection in the mirror. I ran my hands over my face, pushing the long stringy hair away from my eyes. My eyelashes were crusted and glued together from day-old mascara. I attempted to rub it off, but it smudged—great, now I looked like a vampire! I pulled up my sleeve and looked at the fresh needle marks on my arm. They were raw and sore. I spit on my finger and rubbed the blood-streaked puncture wounds.

I was a "shooter." I had been putting drugs in my veins for a long time. However, it never occurred to me that some of the needles I shared were infected with Hepatitis B. Now I was carrying the deadly virus in my body and it was slowly destroying my liver. The resulting jaundice was evident through the sickly yellow tint of my skin and eyes. I never felt good; I had a constant dull ache on my right side and most of the time I was fatigued. I was undernourished. My body was thin and frail; my skin hung on my bones like a draped sheet.

Repulsed, I slammed the visor shut!

"Maybe this wasn't a good idea after all," I blurted out.

"Does that mean you want to leave?" Richard asked anxiously, his hand on the key, ready to start the car.

"No, wait," I mumbled.

"I wish you would make up your mind; go or stay— which one is it?"

I shook my head, trying to clear my jumbled thoughts, and took a deep breath. "Okay," I said, "I'm ready; let's go!" I opened the door and stepped out. My legs hurt, and I could barely stand on them.

Richard came around the car. "You okay?" he asked. "You don't look so good."

I steadied myself and replied, "I'm fine."

"You might want to close the front of your shirt, you're hanging out."

I looked down and sure enough, my breasts were exposed. I tugged at my dirty shirt in an attempt to cover them, but to no avail, it just popped open again. "Hey, if these people don't like the way I am dressed, too bad," I snapped.

Richard tossed his half-smoked cigarette to the ground and grabbed my hand. "You're fine. Let's get this over with!"

We dragged our feet through the parking lot to the entrance and went in. The crowd was enormous; people were walking around in all directions. Some were hugging each other and saying weird things like "Praise the Lord."

Richard had a quirky look on his face. "These people are freaks," he whispered.

We began looking through the crowd for a sign of Linda Smith; she was nowhere in sight. I could feel people staring at me as they passed us by. I stared back at them with cold eyes that reflected "nothingness."

I Am an Addict

Yes, I was a drug addict and it didn't happen overnight. It took me ten long years to achieve that status. My drug of choice was anything and everything; if you had it, I would take it. By mouth, in the arm or up the nose—did not matter. My most frequently used word when getting high was "more." Pot, heroin, coke, meth, pills—they ruled my life!

This driving madness possessed me every hour of every day. My arms were a graveyard of collapsed veins and rock-hard calluses. Each day, like a dog returning to its vomit, I performed the same ritual. First, I put the powder into a spoon, added a little water, and then put a flame under the spoon to dissolve it. Then I drew it into the syringe. Meticulously, I searched my arms, hands and feet for an entrance. It was difficult because my veins were so badly damaged. When I found one, I pierced my flesh with the needle and watched hungrily as the syringe emptied into my arm. My blood stream was like a rushing river that carried the dope to my brain. Upon impact, I was breathless—what dopers refer to as a "rush." And it was pure ecstasy! Every fiber of my being was drenched in an indescribable warm liquid high. I was completely oblivious to the world around me ... in the no-pain zone! The downside? In a few hours, the drug would lose its effect, which meant that I would be back out on the streets searching for ... more!

The Grim Reaper

Wherever there is drug addiction, the Grim Reaper is stationed close by, waiting patiently for his next victim. He knows it is only a matter of time. I have seen him a few times. Once, he was lurking in a dark corner of the room, watching me as I collapsed to the floor after injecting too much heroin.

He wears a floor-length black cloak with a pointed hood pulled over his head. Around his waist is a belt made of rope. His face is a human skull, void of skin or muscle, and his eyes are empty black sockets. His feet and hands are skeletal. In his hand is a sickle; it has a long wooden handle. At the end of it is a razor-sharp blade. His voice is ominous; when he speaks, it sounds like he is talking through a hollow tube. His words are threatening: "Soon you will be mine! Then I will take you to hell, where suffering is eternal!" His laughter is bone chilling.

He is Mr. Death!

At times, the sight of him gripped me with fear. At other times, I challenged him. "Go ahead, take me. I am not afraid of dying!"

"In time, my pretty, in time," he cackled as he slipped away into the darkness from whence he came.

The Reaper's Victims

I knew countless people who died because of drugs. Addicts reaching for the ultimate high inject a lethal amount into their veins, and the next thing you know, they are on the floor, dead as a doornail! The majority of drug dealers are murderers and they have no conscience. Greedy for more money, they cut the drugs with dangerous fillers. Unfortunately, some poor addict in a hurry to get high doesn't taste it. Once it is injected, well, then it's too late!

I knew a guy named Billy, who gave his young girlfriend a shot of what he thought was heroin. She flew against the wall and went into convulsions. Then she lay still in a heap on the floor with her tongue hanging out. Billy stood over her in shock. She looked up at him with a death stare, her eyes wide open. Turns out the drug was cut with battery acid.

Violence lives on the streets where drugs are sold. All too often, the exchange turns ugly and somebody winds up getting wacked (killed). However, that never stopped me from wandering into these dangerous neighborhoods to get drugs. I did whatever it took and never gave it a thought that I was risking my life. When I got the drugs, I took off out of there as fast as I could. The sound of gunshots or an addict lying on the curb, wounded and begging for help, didn't slow me up. I just kept going, leaving the suffering and death behind me. Clutching my drugs as if they were gold, I pressed on in search of a public john where I could put the stuff into my starving vein.

"Another One Bites the Dust"

I can't count the many times I was informed of a car

accident that claimed the life of someone I knew, and it was often related to drugs.

My friend Pam was one who didn't die in the accident but wished she had. While partying one night, she and her boyfriend, Jeff, accepted a ride home with a guy that was stoned out of his mind. He couldn't walk or talk—the guy looked like a zombie. The car they were riding in was traveling at a death-defying speed, on a slick rain-soaked highway. Pam and Jeff were in the back seat smoking crack. Without warning, the car skidded out of control. It lurched from side to side, hit a guardrail and shot out into an open field. In that wide-open field, there was but one solitary tree, just one, and the car was headed right for it ...

At impact, the driver hit the windshield; he was killed instantly! The doors flew open and Pam and Jeff were ejected out of the car. They went sailing through the air like rag dolls and hit the earth with a thud.

The dewy wet landscape was now dotted with two mangled bodies. The creatures of the night fell silent as the sound of groaning was heard from the injured and dying. Ambulance sirens roared, rushing to the scene of the accident, their red lights flashing. Police marched through the high grass with glaring flashlights in search of the victims.

Three people got into the car that night. Only one survived.

When I walked into the intensive care unit to visit Pam, I was shocked at her appearance. She suffered a ruptured spleen, liver damage, as well as broken arms and legs. After a long hospital stay, followed by months of therapy, Pam was released. But she was never the same. Sadly, a few years later, she died of an overdose.

There is an old song "Another One Bites the Dust." The song rang through my head at her funeral; she was twenty-two years old.

Funerals

I hated funerals with a passion! I used to tell my friends, "Listen, when I'm dead, just toss me in a dumpster and make it simple." For me, viewing a dead person is morbid. Therefore, in order to attend, I had to get pretty stoned ... and Pam's funeral was no exception.

The putrid scent of the embalming fluid made me sick and the place reeked of it. I crept over to a chair in a corner to hide, hoping I would be invisible. Watching and listening to the family wail was disturbing. Even worse was the sight of a distraught mother with her body draped over the casket, sobbing.

After hiding in a corner for as long as I could, I got the courage to make my way to the coffin to pay my last respects. Lying on a bed of satin with her head resting on a soft pillow was the shell of someone I once knew. As I viewed her lifeless figure, I asked myself the same question over and over again: *When I'm dead, will anyone weep for me?*

R.I.P.

After the viewing, I followed the slow procession of cars to the cemetery. While the others walked over to the gravesite, I sat in my car with the windows open, listening to the eulogy. The priest read a bible verse, then turned to the family and assured them that their dearly departed was now at "eternal rest."

When it was over and the last car had left the cemetery, I sat alone. That is when I spotted him standing behind one of the tombstones, carving a new notch into the wooden handle of his sickle: the Grim Reaper. His sardonic laughter filled my head.

"Eternal rest for the dead," I murmured, "I doubt it!"

Linda Finally Shows Up

Richard and I were getting antsy, standing around waiting for Linda to show up; besides, the big crowd made us super paranoid.

Richard was ready to leave. "Okay, Carol, where is your friend Linda? I thought you said she was going to be here to meet us." He yanked on my hand, "Come on, let's get out of here. These people are a bunch of loonies and this place gives me the creeps!"

I agreed and we headed for the door. Just as we were about to exit, I heard someone call my name.

"Carol, over here!"

I whirled around. It was Linda! She came rushing over, smiling from ear to ear. She hugged us both and then led us through the crowd to a row of empty seats. After we were seated, she explained the order of the service.

"The music will begin in about an hour—"

Richard interrupted her. "Wait a minute, *an hour* before this thing starts? Then why are we here so early?"

"Richard, this speaker draws a big crowd, so I wanted you to get here early enough to secure a seat."

There was aggravation written all over my husband's face, and to be honest, I was not keen on the hour-long wait either.

What the Heck Kind of Place is This?

Linda suggested we walk around before the service started and meet some of her friends. I assured her that we were fine sitting there but insisted that she should go ahead. As soon as she walked off, Richard got up.

"Carol, I feel weird. I am going out for a smoke. Do you want to come along?"

"Why are you leaving?" I whined.

"If you think I am sitting here for an hour, you're crazy," he replied.

Before I could say another word, he was out the door.

With nothing else to do, I looked around the building. It was very modern. The carpets were colorful and the seats were padded. It looked more like a conference hall. *This is a strange church*, I thought. It did not have any statues or a crucifix with Jesus hanging on it. Instead of an altar, there was a platform with musical instruments and a Plexiglas podium. I wondered if this was not some sort of a cult.

I had only attended one church in my life and it was when I was nine years old. It was a massive old stone building with huge hand-carved wooden doors. Posted on each side of the entrance was a marble angel, each holding a bowl of "holy water." It was customary upon entering or leaving the church to dip your finger in the water and make the "sign of the cross." Inside the dimly lit building, ornate lamps hung down from the high cathedral ceiling. At the front of the church was a lavishly adorned, gold and ivory altar. Over this costly altar hung a large wooden cross, upon which was placed a plaster depiction of Jesus. He had wounds painted on his hands and feet, and there was a hole in his side with blood coming out.

God Answers Prayer?

I was taught that when I prayed, "He" heard me and would answer my prayer. I was also taught that He was everywhere and saw everything. So if I sinned, I risked falling into His wrath!

Knowing this, I strove to be good, because I wanted God to answer my desperate prayers. I not only prayed, I prayed with passion and deep conviction. I pleaded with God to put a stop to the violent fights between my parents. I prayed that we would have more food to eat. I pleaded with Him to heal my dad's mental problems and depression.

Sometimes, as I knelt on the hard pew, I would beg for forgiveness for letting that man sexually abuse me. I knew I could not tell anyone because he would just deny it. Therefore, I cried out to God. I was ashamed and I felt dirty. I wanted God to make me feel clean again.

My most fervent prayer was for my mother. I prayed that the ice around her heart would be shattered and that she could learn to love me.

For one whole year, I hung onto the promise that God hears and answers prayers. I waited for changes that never came. I concluded that my prayers were not heard by God or that He just didn't care!

God is Dead!

One warm spring morning after mass, I sat on the pew and stared up at the cross above the altar. "How can a dead man hear my prayers?" I whispered.

I had sent so many faithful prayers up to heaven, but they were ignored. I couldn't hold back the tears; they came gushing out of my eyes and pouring down my face.

My humility and brokenness suddenly turned to bitterness and rage. I addressed "Him" with burning questions. *If you are God and you see everything, do you see me eating out of garbage cans because there is not enough food at home? And, when my father's belt tears the skin off my legs, doesn't that bother you?*

I buried my head in my hands and cried.

Then I stood to my feet, raised my clenched fists toward heaven and uttered this defiant prayer:

*From now on, I will not depend on you for anything! I am going to make my own rules, and whatever it takes to survive, I'm going to do it! You are not a savior; you don't care about my soul. So, as of right now, my **soul is for sale** and I intend to sell it to the highest bidder!*

I grabbed my sweater off the pew and stormed out of the church.

Meet Linda Smith

Linda and I met at the Poets Lounge, where I worked as a waitress and she was the nighttime disc jockey. From the first time I laid eyes on her, I sensed she was "different." The girl was just too nice! In addition, she did not hang out with the crew after hours, and although drugs flowed through the place like a river, she stayed clear of them. She shunned gossip and never used foul language. Strange! Besides that, she was a knockout and could have had her pick of any man in the place, but every night she went home to her husband, to the dismay of all the men who lusted after her.

So why was a girl like that working in a cheaters' bar? Curious, I posed the question to the bartender.

"Hey Ray, what goes with Linda? She is so straight!"

He laughed. "Haven't you heard? Linda is religious."

I was surprised. "Really? Tell me, how does God feel about her working in a bar?"

"I don't know; if you're interested, why don't you go over and ask her?" Ray suggested.

I shook my head and replied, "No thanks, I don't need to hear any of that religious crap."

Weeping Waitresses

On the job, Linda never tried to shove her "religion" down anyone's throat. Good thing, because I did not want to hear it, and I was prepared to tell her off if she started talking that jive mess to me! Still, she intrigued me, so I watched her from afar.

One night I overheard her talking to one of the waitresses. The girl's name was Leah. Seems Leah had an affair with one of the customers who frequented the Lounge. Her husband got wind of it, slapped her around and then filed for a divorce. Leah was crying as she explained to Linda how it all happened.

"Working in a place like this makes it hard to be faithful, Linda," Leah explained. "Everyone is drinking and partying. One thing leads to another and before you know it, you're doing things you regret, only by that time it is too late."

I pretended I was busy, but believe me, I was listening to every word.

"You must think I am an awful person," Leah sobbed.

Linda corrected her, "No, I don't!"

"Will you pray for my marriage, Linda?"

"You can count on it, Leah," Linda assured her.

As I watched this drama unfold, I wanted to laugh out loud. *Give me a break, what a crock! Prayer is a joke and Linda is a Jesus freak*, I thought to myself.

Though I felt like the whole prayer thing was a waste of time, most of the girls that worked in the Lounge didn't agree, and they genuinely liked Linda. None of them hesitated to come to her for prayer, advice or a shoulder to cry on. On any given night, before the place got busy, you might see Linda off in a corner listening intently as one of the girls poured their heart out to her. Linda did not repeat things entrusted to her, and in a place like Poets Lounge, that was major!

Ray

Ray was the bartender. He was a handsome guy with a smile that boasted rows of pretty white teeth. We worked together on the night shift. We shared stories, jokes, insults and drugs. As time went on, we became good friends and we looked out for each other. When Ray lost his license for drunk driving, I made the long trip to drive him home after work at four in the morning. When my car broke down in a rainstorm, he was the one who crawled underneath and got it running again.

Ray loved to mock people, so I found it surprising how he would jump to Linda's defense when I made fun of her. For example, I noticed between sets, she had her eyes closed and her lips moving. Thus, I brought it to Ray's attention.

"Hey, check out Linda. I think she's up there praying. She's a strange bird!"

Instead of joining in, he responded, "Carol, I need all the prayer I can get, and by the way, so do you!"

Ray, I Think I Am Dying

Some weekdays, Ray and I would volunteer to work the lunch shift. One afternoon, following a busy lunch hour, we finished our chores and stood around in the waitress station, drinking coffee and chatting. I noticed he was staring at my face.

"What the heck are you looking at?" I asked.

"You look like you have lost weight and your skin is a funny yellow color. You feeling all right?"

I ignored his question, but my pensive behavior only stirred his curiosity.

He pressed on for an answer. "Well, Carol, are you going to tell me? Is something wrong?"

I took a deep breath and answered, "I have Hepatitis B. My skin color is a symptom of it. The doctor said my liver is drying up."

Ray set his coffee cup down on the counter and leaned in to get a closer look. "Yeah, I noticed it about a week ago; the whites of your eyes are really yellow."

"Yes, I know. Besides that, I have peptic bleeding ulcers."

He looked surprised. "When did you find all this out?"

"I had tests; the doctor called and talked to Richard," I answered.

"So, what are they going to do for you?"

"I'm not sure. They have this new medicine that helps to heal ulcers, but the liver thing is very serious." I looked around to make sure no one was listening; this sort of thing could have cost me my job. "Ray, you can't tell anyone about this!"

"I won't," he promised, "but I suggest you lay off the hard stuff or you're going to land up six feet under."

A Night at Poets

It was Saturday night at Poets Lounge. Every table in the place was taken and people were five deep at the bar. The sound of music, laughter, and buzzing conversation filled the place. On the dance floor, couples were swaying to the beat of the music. Linda was up in her box playing piped-in music between the live band sets.

I spent half the night in the john doing lines. I'd come waltzing out with white powder lacing the inside of my nostrils and my eyes bugging out. Still, I kept up with the demands for drinks and food that were coming at me with rapid speed. My feet would have been killing me, given the exhaustive work, but the cocaine kept me numb.

I signaled to Ray, letting him know that I had left a stash for him in the bathroom. He disappeared for a few minutes and then returned, buzzing from his "coke jolt."

Somewhere around four in the morning, he made "last call." It was time to get the people out the door and clean up the place.

When I finished prepping my station, I sat down. I slipped off my shoes, poured my tips out on the table and started counting. Ray was finishing up behind the bar. I called over to him, "Ray, make me a 151 rum and coke, will ya?"

"You don't need a drink, Carol; you're wasted, and besides, the insides of your nose are snow white."

"Just give me a drink, Ray," I insisted.

He made the drink and slid it across the bar to me. "You better take it easy," he warned.

Linda Makes Her Move

About this time, Linda came strolling over. She had a steaming cup of coffee in her hand and a big smile. "So, did you make out good in tips tonight?" she asked.

"I did all right," I answered. "I thought you'd be on your way home by now, Linda," I said, hoping she'd go away.

"Do you mind if I sit down for a minute?"

I told her it was okay, but I was lying. I wanted her to get lost. I tucked my money into my purse and took a swig of my drink.

"You look tired, Carol; are you okay?"

"How do you mean?" I asked suspiciously.

She moved her chair closer to mine. It made me uncomfortable. "Well, I heard you're sick and I wondered if I could help."

I felt like someone sucked the air out of the room. "Who told you that?" I bellowed.

She looked over to the bar where Ray was cleaning up. I thought I was going to blow a blood vessel. She reached over to touch my hand; I pulled it away.

"Carol," she said tenderly, "I've been praying for you."

"Listen here, Linda," I said, my voice dripping with venom, "I don't want or need your stupid prayers. I'm not one of these flunky waitresses who cry on your shoulder. My life is none of your business!" I raised my glass in the air with a mock toast, finished the contents and slammed it down on the table.

Betrayed

I stood up, grabbed my purse and shoes, and left her sitting there. "And a good night to you too, blabbermouth!" I shouted to Ray as I stormed out.

In the parking lot, I fumbled with my car keys, opened the car door and jumped in. I was shaken to the core. "Who does Linda think she is?" I mumbled, "And Ray selling me out? It's a freaking conspiracy; those jokers are going to get me fired!"

I drove down the road, pressing the pedal to the floor. I ran a red light and hit the curb. Finally, I pulled over. I couldn't think straight. I reached in my purse and pulled out my stash. I sent a load up my nose. The drug hit me fast and hard. But it didn't make me feel any better.

"Why won't people just leave me alone?" I whimpered, "I don't want to be rescued."

I pounded my head on the steering wheel. The harder I slammed, the better it felt. The pain I inflicted was more bearable than the pain in my heart. I felt a warm liquid trickling down my forehead; I wiped it with the back of my hand, spreading blood all over my face.

The Kiss of Death

Ray had betrayed me and it hurt.

The next afternoon, I put a lot of dope in my vein. As soon as the stuff got in my system, I knew it was too much. The room started spinning. I could not catch my breath. I grabbed the tub and slid down to the floor. I could feel the drug running through my body, slowing down the functions. My heart was beating very slowly and my breathing was shallow. I decided to relax and let it happen.

As I tumbled down into the abyss, I could hear a faint voice in the distance calling my name, pleading with me to "come back!" Someone was shaking me and forcing me to walk. My heart picked up its pace and I could breathe again. I just barely opened my eyes and saw my husband standing over me.

"Carol, I thought I lost you. I was sure this time you weren't coming back!" He lifted me up, carried me to the bedroom, and gently laid me down on the bed. "We have got to stop living like this! You almost died ..." His words were etched with emotion.

My tongue felt thick; I could barely speak. "I'm okay, Richard," I whispered. Within minutes, I fell into a deep sleep.

When I woke up, Richard was not there. I kept seeing the look on his face, sheer panic. I knew this time I had really scared him, but truthfully, I wished he had let me die.

My Grandfather Died (Again!)

My liver hurt, my joints ached and I had a horrendous pounding headache. I called the manager to get out of going to work.

"Kenny, my grandfather died. I have to go to the funeral." I was trying to sound grief-stricken.

"I thought you said he died a few months ago."

"No, that was my other grandfather," I argued.

"Yeah, but last year you told me your grandfather died too," he argued back.

I knew that he was at his wits end with my excuses.

"Okay, Carol, I know you're lying. You got three days off. After that, you'd better get your butt in here or you're out of a job, you understand?" He slammed the phone down in my ear.

Three days went by quickly, but I knew if I did not get back to work, I would be fired. So I pulled myself together and went in. When I strolled into the waitress station to get ready for the busy night, Ray spotted me and came over.

"Hey, I heard your grandfather died, *again*. Let me see, is that the fourth or fifth time?"

"Ha, ha, very funny." I was annoyed that he was amused.

He didn't stop. "Carol, I suggest you start killing off your grandmothers if you're going to ask for time off!"

Ray was funny, and he had a point. I gave in and laughed with him. That broke the ice between us over the Linda thing. Nevertheless, later that night, I confronted him about it.

"Ray, why did you tell Linda what I told you? You know that if management gets wind of my condition, I will be out of a job."

He began his defense. "Listen, Carol, I was just trying to help. Linda doesn't repeat things; she would never put your job in jeopardy."

I questioned him, "How did you think she was going to help me?"

"I don't know; I guess I thought she might pray for you," he answered sheepishly.

"Are you nuts, Ray? Prayer is a joke and so is she!" I turned and stomped off.

Something the Cat Dragged In

Three nights later, on my day-off, I wandered into the Lounge. I was stoned out of my mind. I was wearing a pair of slinky black pants that had slits down both legs, a glittery gold tube top that barely covered my breasts, and oversized hoop earrings to finish off my ensemble. My arm was streaked with blood, and my mouth was stained with dried saliva. I looked like something the cat dragged in.

I stood at the door, teetering on my stiletto heels. Someone tapped me on my shoulder; it was Linda.

"Hey Carol," she was shouting to be heard above the loud music, "are you okay?"

I smiled smugly and walked past her. Ray saw me coming toward the bar and came right over.

"Man, Carol, you look wired! You need to go home and sleep it off."

I glared at him. "Give me a vodka and orange juice."

He leaned over the bar. "You don't need a drink."

"I am a paying customer tonight, and I want a drink, Ray!"

He poured a glass of orange juice, topped it off with a dribble of vodka, then brought it over and set it down in front of me.

"I asked for a drink, Ray, not an O.J."

He looked me up and down. "What exactly are you dressed for? It's a bit early for a Halloween costume, wouldn't you say?" he snickered and walked away.

Mistaken For a Prostitute

I pushed the drink across the bar and left.

Outside, I stood in the middle of the parking lot, looking around for my car. I could not remember if I drove there or if I was dropped off.

I started walking down the highway, heading towards a bar up the street. It was a dark black night, not a star in the sky. I felt a raindrop and then it started to pour.

I tripped and fell headfirst into a ditch filled with water and mud. I hit my head on the side of the hole. Immediately, a bump formed on my forehead. I was feeling dizzy from the fall, so I plopped down on the curb. I had broken off the heel of one of my shoes and was fumbling to try to reattach it.

I was blinded by headlights; a car pulled up. It stopped and I heard a man's voice.

"Hey honey, I am looking for a good time. You working tonight?"

"I'm no prostitute, you moron!" I shouted at him.

"Well if you're not, you sure look like one," he retorted as he took off, spinning his tires and sending a blast of mud and gravel in my face.

I slowly got up on my feet, still wobbling with the broken heel, and tried to walk. I had lost all sense of direction.

Again, bright headlights blinded me. This time, it was not the guy looking for a good time; it was the cops. An officer got out of the patrol car and approached me.

"Lady, what are you doing wandering the streets at four o'clock in the morning? Let me see your I.D."

I was dazed and confused, but managed to reply, "I think I lost my purse, Officer."

He took me by the arm and led me to the car, put me in the back seat, and took me over to the local precinct. When he put me in a cell to sleep it off, I went crazy.

"Why are you locking me up, you freaking jerk? You are infringing on my rights. I didn't break any laws."

"Shut that hole in your face," the officer ordered, "before I ship you downtown."

I continued to rant, peppering my insults with obscenities. Within an hour, I was transferred downtown to the holding center for prostitutes.

A Night With the "Girls"

I woke to the sound of shuffling and movement. I was lying on a cold concrete floor. My head was throbbing and I had a big lump on my forehead. My clothes were covered in dried mud and I only had one shoe on. I heard a female voice addressing me.

"Come on, honey," the voice cooed, "we know you're holding, and we know where you got 'em hid."

I rubbed my eyes and tried to focus. I was surrounded by a bunch of prostitutes. The taller girl got down on the floor next to me. I could smell her cheap cologne. She pressed her greasy face against mine. I turned my head in the other direction.

"I am not holding, and I don't have any drugs hidden in my body crevices," I told her.

She kept it up. "Girl, unless you haven't noticed, you are all alone in here, and I could put a hurting on you!"

I had no doubt that she could easily hurt me; she was much bigger and stronger. However, this was not the first time that I was confronted by someone who was threatening to beat me up. I learned early on that you never back down; it might mean that you are going down, but you never show fear!

I pulled myself up off the floor, took a deep breath and stood tall. I glared directly into her eyes. "Now, you listen to me," I declared boldly, "like I said, I ain't holding, and I don't scare easy, so back off!"

I was expecting her to nail me; instead, she stood there

staring me down—still, I did not flinch!

In the corner, sitting against the wall, was a woman; she let out a howl, exposing a mouth of rotted teeth, and then said, "Oh my, this little white girl ain't scared of you, Jessica. No way, she is standing right up to you!"

The girl backed off. A few minutes later, my name was called and I was released.

Shut Up, Ray

When word got around the Lounge that I had been picked up for loitering and jailed with prostitutes for the night, I became the brunt of all the jokes. A few times, I threatened to punch someone in the face if they didn't lay off.

"Don't get so mad, Carol," Ray chuckled, "you landed up in the tank with a herd of prostitutes. People are going to rib you about it, so just take it in stride."

As for Linda, the church lady, I had both guns loaded if she dared to approach me. I intended to ward her off with more four-letter words than she had heard in a lifetime.

Strangely, she never said a word about it.

Ray kidded me though. "Hey, Carol, I think Linda has increased her prayers for you since your night in the clink."

I was angry and defensive. "Buddy, if anyone here needs prayer, it's you!"

Ray's voice turned serious. "Yes, you're absolutely right! I have a lot of issues, but I'm not the one who is dying, am I?"

Supernatural Power

One night when leaving the Lounge after work, I spotted Linda in the parking lot. I pretended not to see her and quickly got into my car. I started the engine and began to pull away, but a tapping on the window startled me. I looked up; she was peering through the glass.

I rolled down the window and asked, "What do you want, Linda? I am in a hurry."

"Carol, I just wanted to invite you to one of our Friday-night services."

I started to close the window and replied, "No thanks."

She put her hand out to stop it from going up. "There are people getting healed by God."

"*Getting healed?*" I mocked. "Linda, you must know how crazy you sound!"

She stepped back. "Do I, Carol? You're involved in witchcraft and you operate in supernatural power, right? What's so hard to believe that God can and does heal people?" she asked.

I forced the window closed and drove away, leaving her standing there.

After that encounter, Linda barely talked to me. She was cordial but distant, and believe it or not, it bothered me!

Ray noticed and commented, "Did you and Linda have a falling-out?"

"What makes you think that?"

"Well, she usually has coffee with us, and she hasn't come near the waitress station lately."

Okay, I will go!

A week later, I strolled over to the disc jockey box. Linda was busy putting things up for the night. She turned around and I was standing there.

"I have decided to come to one of your meetings."

She raised her eyebrows and asked, "Oh really?"

"Well, I am interested in the supernatural. I have read about witch doctors that can heal people. I also studied Edgar Cayce. He fell into trances and diagnosed illnesses. I'm intrigued with that sort of thing."

Linda seemed amused at my comments. "Okay, the church is on Union Road in Orchard Park. I would suggest you get there about six." She smiled and went back to what she was doing.

If I was expecting her to jump for joy over my decision to attend one of her "religious meetings," I was wrong; she didn't.

CHAPTER TWO

In the Eyes of a Child – My Past Revisited

Take the Money and Run

Sitting on the pew and waiting for the service to begin, I felt my body start to shake. Linda was bopping around the church in high gear, talking to people. Richard was still gone; I wasn't even sure if he'd be coming back. I was beginning to squirm. I knew it wouldn't be long before I would need "something" and the drugs were in the car. I was bored, fidgety and ready to leave.

On the seat beside me was a bible with Linda's name embossed on it. I thumbed through the pages; she had highlighted several of the sentences. I tried to read some of it, but the thee's and thou's confused me, so I tossed it back on the seat.

That's when I saw it—just a few feet away—a purse with a wallet sticking out. Immediately, I was consumed with temptation. This would be the perfect opportunity to get some extra cash to buy drugs.

But this is a church and people don't steal in churches, do they?

I began reasoning with myself. *If that person is stupid enough to leave a purse unattended with a thousand people walking around, then they deserve to have it stolen.*

Furthermore, who would suspect me anyway? I would be long gone before it was discovered missing. As for Linda, she would assume I got tired of waiting and took off.

So, it was settled; I would steal the wallet and leave!

I slid over and placed my hand next to the purse. I tapped my fingers and looked around to see if anyone was watching. The coast was clear! I reached into the purse and took hold of the wallet; I tightened my grip and began to pull it out. It was coming out smoothly; I almost had it, just one more tug!

Suddenly, I felt someone's eyes on me. A sick feeling formed in the pit of my stomach. Oh no, I was busted! How was I going to explain this? I pulled back my hand, took a deep breath and lifted my head.

Sitting directly in front of me, peering over the pew, was a little girl. Man, was I relieved! There was no way the kid knew that I was planning to lift the wallet. I smiled sweetly and slid back into my original seat.

An older woman was seated next to her. "Madison, turn around and don't bother the lady."

"I'm not bothering her, Grandma," the little girl replied, "I'm just looking at her."

Where is Your Mommy?

"Your name is Madison. That's a pretty name," I said, trying to sound like a nice woman instead of a thief.

"Thank you," she replied politely. "I am here with my mommy. She went to the bathroom. Are you here with your mommy?"

"No, I am with my husband and some friends," I told her.

"What is your name, and where is your mommy?"

"My name is Carol, and I don't know where my mother is," I answered abruptly.

"Oh, aren't you sad that your mommy is not here with you?" she asked with a sad voice.

Before I could answer, a woman came over and sat down.

"I was talking to this lady, Mommy. Her name is Carol and her mommy didn't come with her."

"I hope she didn't disturb you," the woman said apologetically.

I shook my head and responded, "No, not at all."

"My name is Nicole. Is this your first time here?"

"Yes, it is," I answered.

"Well, I do hope you enjoy the service." She turned back around and pulled Madison close to her. I could hear her whispering in her daughter's ear, "I love you, baby."

I could not help but wonder what it feels like to be so young and know you are loved by the most important person in the world—your mother.

As I watched the display of love between a mother and daughter, Madison's question echoed in my mind. *Aren't you sad that your mommy is not here with you?*

I traveled back in my mind to the first time I felt …

The Absence of Love

I woke up to the sound of my mother's harsh voice; it was shouting, "Carol, get up and get ready!"

I was five years old and supposed to register at the local

school on this day. I dressed quickly. I stood on my tiptoes and looked into the bathroom mirror. I had a few flyaway hairs sticking up, so I licked my fingers and ran them over the top of my head to smooth them down. When I was finished, I rushed into the kitchen to eat my bowl of cereal. Mom came in shooting orders at my sister Joanne.

"By the time I get back, I want this house cleaned. I have to walk Carol to the school, so it will be awhile. Keep your eyes on the kids."

Mom stood at the back door and held it open. "Well, don't just stand there; let's go!"

She jerked me out the door and we began the quarter-mile walk to the school. I could hardly keep up; Mom was pregnant but she sure did walk fast. By the time we got there, my legs ached. We went through the big doors and started down the long hallway. I attempted to peek into the classrooms, but Mom was moving fast and instructing me to "come along."

I Am Dorothy Thompson, and I Will be First!

When we reached the registration desk, the teacher instructed the parents to line their children against the wall in single file and wait for their names to be called.

Mom strutted up to the woman in charge and proceeded to tell her that she would not be waiting like the others. "I have babies at home, and as you can see, I am pregnant. I will have to go first."

The woman looked at my very pregnant mother and addressed her sternly. "Ma'am, there are plenty of mothers here this morning that are in a hurry; each is waiting her turn, and you will have to do the same."

That didn't go over well. First, no one talked to Dorothy Thompson that way or in that tone. Second, she did not take no for an answer.

Thus, she repeated herself. "As I said, I am pregnant and I have babies at home. Now, you will kindly take Carol first and let me get out of here!"

The woman cleared her throat; her tension was obvious to all. "Okay, Mrs. Thompson, under the circumstances, I will permit your child to be first."

My mother moved me to the front of the line, shoved me against the wall and ordered me to stand there until I was taken to the classroom.

"I will be back to pick you up."

"Where are you going, Mommy?" I asked, my voice shaking.

"Home, where else?" she answered coldly.

I started to worry. "Mommy, wait, I want you to stay here with me."

"Stop it! I can't stay, and I haven't time for this!" She turned and walked out without looking back. The door made a loud banging sound when it slammed shut.

A feeling of abandonment came over me. I wiped my tears with the back of my hand. I was the only child left alone, and *I was sad that my mommy was not there with me.*

Rats, Trains and a Meddling Old Woman

Memories, such as the one I just described, began when I was just five years old. At the time, we lived on Elk Street, in a place on the "other side of the tracks." The rambling old house was next to a dirty railroad yard that was infested with rats. The big ugly critters nested there and some of them took up residence in our apartment. It was not unusual to find their droppings in the flour or cereal. Sometimes you could catch a glimpse of one scurrying across the floor into a hole in the wall or under a couch.

The trains went thundering by at least twice a day. The sound of their loud whistles pierced the air. They shook the dishes in the cabinets, and I could feel the floor trembling beneath my feet.

My great-grandmother lived in the apartment above us. However, she spent a great deal of time downstairs with us, helping my pregnant mother with cooking and raising five kids.

Great-Grandma was an ornery old widow with a sharp tongue. She was a full-blooded Polish woman from the old country who was not afraid to speak her mind. She nagged my father about my mother being pregnant every other year. "Why don't you try keeping your pants up, Tom?" she scolded him. "Your wife is too young to be having all these babies; it's taking a toll on her health! Now she is pregnant again. Leave her be, you hear me?"

The old woman was way out of line and Dad resented it, but he kept his mouth shut and turned a tin ear to her. To escape the nagging "in-law," he saved a down payment and started looking around for a house to buy. There was a new development going up about ten miles away in the town of Cheektowaga. He and my mother decided on a little ranch with three bedrooms. They went to the bank and made all the arrangements, but it would be months before the house was finished and they could move in, so they decided not to mention it to anyone.

A Night of Blood and Death

We were still living in the old house when I woke up one night to a blood-curdling scream. It was coming from my parents' bedroom.

When I sat up in my bed, I saw Great-Grandma go rushing by and heard her ask, "Dorothy, what is it? What is wrong?"

My mother was sitting up in the bed. She was pale and the sheets were bloody. I grabbed my sister's arm; we were both trembling.

Great-Grandma shooed us away from the door. "You kids get back to bed!"

However, we could not move.

Mom let out a groan and then fell back on the pillow.

Great-Grandma picked up a lamp, removed the shade, threw back the covers and shined the light down between my mother's legs. "Oh my God!" she shrieked.

Lying there in a pool of blood was a baby. He was hanging halfway out of my mother's body. The sight of it made my heart pound. I didn't understand what was happening. I knew Mom had a baby inside her tummy and that was why it was big. Yet, the sight of the baby lying there terrified me.

"Oh my God, take it out!" my mother cried.

Great-Grandma left the room and then returned with pair of scissors and a washcloth. I watched as she cut something and then wrapped the tiny baby in the washcloth.

"Is my baby dead?"

"Yes, child, he is."

Mom balled her fist up and began beating the bed. She cried, "Why? What happened?"

"You had a miscarriage, Dorothy. The little boy came too

33

soon. You need to hold him before I take him away. This will be the last time you will see him."

My mother stared in disbelief. She reached out and took the washcloth that held her baby. Tears filled her eyes. "He's so little, my poor little baby boy!"

Great-Grandma gathered up the blood-soaked sheets. She carried them down to the basement and then returned. "Okay, Dorothy, it's time to take him away."

Mom was crying and rocking back and forth.

"Come on, Dorothy, give him here," Great-Grandma insisted.

"What are you going to do with him?"

The old woman patted her on the head. "Don't you worry; I will take care of it." She took the baby and left the room.

My sister and I crept back into our beds. I closed my eyes and tried to sleep. Hours later, except for the sound of my heart beating in my chest, the house was still.

Your Son is Dead

When Dad came home from work early the next morning, Great-Grandma was waiting for him at the door.

"Your wife lost the baby last night, Tom. It was a boy."

"What happened? Is Dorothy okay?" He made a dash for the bedroom, but the old woman blocked the way.

"Leave her be, Tom. Dorothy is very weak and upset."

His voice shaky, he asked, "Where is the baby?"

Great-Grandma went to the basement and came back with a canning jar in her hand.

"Oh my God, why did you put him in there?" Dad asked in shock.

"What did you expect me to do, Tom, report it? No need to, what is done is done!"

"Just take it out of here before Dorothy sees it," he pleaded.

"She already has," the old woman replied.

Dad pushed past her and headed for the bedroom.

He knelt down beside the bed. "Dorothy," he whispered softly.

Her eyes fluttered.

"Babe, I am so sorry," he said, trying to comfort his young wife.

"Go away, Tom, and leave me alone, please!" she cried, "I don't want to talk about it."

Traumatized

The miscarriage traumatized my mother. She fell into a deep depression and refused to talk to anyone. The only one who could get near her was Great-Grandma.

A few months later, she was pregnant again.

The old woman went after my father, shaking her long bony finger in his face. "Tom, you got Dorothy pregnant again; are you crazy? She just lost a baby and she hasn't had time to heal!"

He shouted right back at her, "Mind your own business! Dorothy is my wife!"

"Yes, she is, but in case you haven't noticed, your wife is miserable! She rarely smiles, and half the time, she's depressed!"

Great-Grandma marched back upstairs, Dad stormed out to get a drink, and my mother went to her room to cry.

A Cold Beer on a Frigid Night

The last winter we spent in the old house on Elk Street was a cold one. The temperatures fell into the teens and we had two major snowstorms. Mom was seven months pregnant and bored. Most nights she sat home in front of the television.

One evening in particular, I remember sitting on my bed, gazing out the window and watching as the snowflakes tumbled down and covered the ground in a white blanket of snow. I could hear my parents talking in the living room.

"Dorothy, mind if I go out for a few beers?" Dad asked.

"Why should I sit here while you go out?" she protested.

"I thought you might want to rest."

"Well, you're wrong, Tom. If you're going, I'm going too!"

She pulled her very pregnant body up off the couch and headed to her room to freshen up. Dad went outside to scrape the ice off the windows and warm up the car. I watched as they drove away into the cold, dark night.

According to My Mother, This is What Transpired

When they got to the bar, it was deserted, except for one other couple. The girl was young and very pretty; she was throwing back shots of tequila. The guy with her was passed out with his head on the bar.

Dorothy noticed her husband staring at the girl.

"What are you looking at?" she snipped. "I sit here pregnant, while you drool over some tramp!"

"Don't be silly, honey; I didn't even notice her."

While they were arguing, the girl danced her way up to the table and asked, "Mind if I borrow your man for a dance or two?"

"No, you can't dance with my husband. Wake up your drunken boyfriend and get him to dance with you," Dorothy told her.

As the girl staggered back to the dance floor, Dorothy got up and headed to the bathroom.

Dirty Dancing

When she came out of the restroom, her jaw dropped. Her husband was dancing with the young girl. His arms were wrapped around her waist and their bodies were pressed together in a sexy embrace. Dorothy stomped over to the dance floor with fire in her eyes.

"Get your hands off my husband before I rearrange your face, you tramp!"

The girl threw her head back and laughed. Dorothy hauled off and punched her in the face, cracking her front tooth. The commotion woke up the drunken boyfriend.

The girl screeched, "That fat heifer broke my damn tooth!"

Tom gathered his wife's belongings and pushed her toward the door. He knew all too well that being pregnant would not stop his wife.

The bartender was amused. "I'm closing in five minutes," he announced; then he turned to the girl and said, "And as for you, young lady, you're lucky Tom took her out of here. That is Dorothy Thompson and *no one* messes with her man. You better thank your lucky stars you got off with just a broken tooth."

White Snow Dotted with Blood

Outside, the argument was escalating. Tom denied

Dorothy's accusations and tried to reason with her, but it was no use—she was convinced otherwise.

"Do you take me for a fool, Tom?"

"Dorothy, it was just a dance, nothing else!"

"You're a liar! You keep me pregnant and out of shape while you sleep with other women!"

"That's not true," he argued.

"Yes it is and you know it!" She was swinging at him wildly.

"Be careful," he cautioned, "these stairs are icy—"

Before the words got out of his mouth, she was falling. He reached for her, but it was too late. His pregnant wife went tumbling down the steps. She landed on her back in the snow. Tom rushed down and knelt beside her. She was wet, cold and wincing in pain. When he tried to lift her, she groaned. The bartender, who had heard the rumpus, came rushing out. Together, they lifted her and placed her in the car. There was a trail of blood dotting the snow. When Tom saw it, he knew that there was a serious problem.

Within hours, Dorothy was in the hospital giving birth to a baby boy, two-and-a-half months early. His little lungs were not completely developed and breathing was a chore for him. There were a few times they were sure he would die.

The agony that Dorothy suffered during those crucial first months cannot be put into words. She prayed that God would spare her son. She refused to lose another boy to a premature birth. After a long stay in the hospital, Cronley was released and came home to his family.

CHAPTER THREE

A Short-Lived Happiness

Our New Life on Colby Street

The house on Colby Street was finished and ready for us to move in.

Dad was elated. Now he could take his wife and children away from the ratty old apartment and his meddling "in-law," to a new home and a fresh start. He beamed as they broke the news to Great-Grandma.

She scowled and warned him to be careful. "A house with just three bedrooms is too tiny for a family of eight."

Dad assured her that it would be fine.

With the car packed and the kids piled in, we drove away from our old life on Elk Street to our new life on Colby Street.

"Stay in the car until I motion you to come in," Dad instructed when he pulled up the driveway of the newly built house. He jumped out of the car, ran to the front door, placed the shiny key into the lock and swung the door open. He then signaled for us to come.

We all jumped out of the car and ran inside; Mom followed close behind with Cronley in her arms. The smell of fresh lumber and paint filled the rooms of the tiny house. We children ran from room to room, shouting and laughing, our voices filled with glee. Dad began envisioning all the new additions he intended to make to improve the house and property.

"I am going to put a playroom in the basement, a swing set in the back yard, and plant a huge vegetable garden, along with lots of trees and flowers," he said excitedly.

Mom walked through the bedrooms trying to figure out which would be the girls' room and which would be the boys' room. She seemed quite content with the new home, and I saw something on her face that was rarely there—a smile.

By summer, the garden was bursting with fresh vegetables, and the rest of the yard was coming together nicely as well. Tulips bloomed in the spring, lilacs in May, and a variety of roses in the summer. Dad remodeled the basement and put up a swing set in the backyard, just as he had planned. Laughter filled the house, food was plentiful, and to top it off, Dad got a raise. One afternoon, he drove up the driveway in a brand new car.

Wow, life was grand and I was a happy kid! It was a time of peace and plenty. I was seven years old and I can say without reservation, "It was well with my soul."

"Dorothy, Something is Wrong with Cronley"

One Fourth of July, we had a party in the back yard. Our aunts and uncles came over with their children. The women were outside, soaking up the rays and watching the kids while keeping an eye on the grill. Down in the cool basement, the men were hooting and howling over their hot poker game. The stakes were high and the beer was flowing. We played with our cousins on the swing set. It was a perfect day. Hot dogs, hamburgers, chicken and steak were sizzling over red-hot coals. The table was laden with scrumptious foods and desserts.

Suddenly, my aunt came out of the house clutching Cronley; she had a puzzled look on her face.

"What is it, Aunt Jean?" Mom asked.

"I am not sure, Dorothy, but I think there is something wrong with Cronley. When I put things in front of his eyes, he acts like he doesn't see them," she explained.

Mom called down to the basement, "Tom, come up here, now!"

Dad came up the stairs in a flash.

All at once, there was total confusion. People were leaning over Cronley and putting things in front of his eyes. Everyone was jabbering and giving their opinion.

Mom looked at Dad; their eyes locked. Something was dreadfully wrong.

The next morning, they took Cronley to the doctor.

After a thorough examination, the doctor concluded, "Mrs. Thompson, Cronley is blind. I would venture to say the premature birth caused it. He did not have sufficient time in the womb for his eyes to finish developing. I am surprised we didn't catch this sooner."

My mother fell into the chair. "What are you saying, Doctor?"

"Well, what I am saying is that your son will require proper care. There is a facility in New Jersey that takes handicapped children."

"No way," Mom protested, getting up from her seat to

leave, "my son will stay at home with his family and we will take care of him. No kid of mine is going into an institution; he is not retarded!"

"Mrs. Thompson," the doctor reasoned, "a handicapped child needs constant care and you have small children. Please consider your options."

My parents left the doctor's office stunned! That night, I could hear them arguing.

"It's your fault, Tom; you were flirting with that tramp on the dance floor that night. That is why I swung at you out on the stairs where I slipped and fell!"

"Don't blame me, Dorothy! It was a terrible accident, but don't put this on me, please!"

They tried to come up with a solution, but they kept coming back to the same conclusion: Cronley would need constant care and an environment that was suitable for his handicap. After much debate, my parents signed the papers.

My Baby Brother, Gone!

It was dark and gloomy the day that Cronley went away. Mom was angry and depressed.

"Honey, please try to settle down; you're pregnant and you need to think about the baby you're carrying," Dad cautioned her.

"I am not thinking about the baby I am pregnant with," she hissed, "I am thinking about my blind son leaving home to live in an institution."

Mom gathered us in the living room to bid farewell to our little brother. Dad's eyes were red and swollen. He watched as each one of us kissed Cronley and said goodbye. My mother's face was expressionless; she was numb.

After we finished our goodbyes, my parents left for the long trip to the institution. It would be my brother's home for the rest of his life.

I stood with my face pressed against the window as the car pulled out of the driveway. I whispered his name, then ran into the bedroom and pulled his blanket out of the crib. I crawled under my bed and pressed it to my cheek. His scent was there, but he was gone. I was only seven years old and my heart was breaking in two. I rolled up in a ball and cried. After what seemed like a very long time, I drifted off to sleep.

Gone and Forgotten?

Cronley would spend the rest of his natural life growing increasingly detached from the real world. His home was the institution; his family, the staff there. The words "mommy" or "daddy" were never understood in his mind. In time, he was medicated for having grand mal seizures. They administered strong drugs to sedate him. My mother was convinced the drugs affected his mind because he eventually became retarded. Cronley lived in a world of his own and died years later in the institution.

His blindness and retardation affected my mother deeply; she never completely recovered from it. Therefore, in order to survive, she erected a wall around her heart, which shielded her from any further pain. However, that wall became a two-edged sword: it not only protected her from any additional injury, but it also kept her children out, as she became increasingly cold and unemotional. Affection, hugs, or words of endearment never left her lips. We spent most of our days dodging her random blows, bad moods and fits of anger.

As the years passed, I became painfully aware that the brunt of her anger and rage would fall on me, a hell from which there seemed to be no escape.

Things Change

After Cronley went away, things changed. The laughter that once filled the rooms of our home was now replaced with bickering and fighting. The dreams my parents had for a happy life were now shattered. Everyone and everything suffered. The garden that once boasted fresh vegetables was now rotted and dry. The roses that burst with color along the borders of the house were wilted, and the lush green grass was now a carpet of ugly weeds. The paint on the house peeled, the swing set rusted, and the basement was in need of repair.

Mom was pregnant with my sister. The thought of carrying another child was overwhelming for her. She was miserable, uncomfortable and visibly unhappy.

To fill the long days and empty hours, my parents resorted to a steady diet of alcohol.

CHAPTER FOUR

All My Joy, Turned to Sorrow

Hungry

*D*ad started complaining of headaches. His vision was blurred and his hands were numb. On the job, he was suffering from fatigue and missing a lot of work.

After a complete checkup, the doctor's diagnosis was "extreme high blood pressure." They warned my mother, "Your husband is a walking time bomb, Mrs. Thompson; his blood pressure is sky-high. He could have a heart attack or stroke at any time."

Mom was frantic. She had a baby on the way, her husband was missing work, and they were running out of money. The bill collectors were ringing the phone off the hook and the mailbox was loaded with reminders.

What was once plentiful was now scarce. Breakfast consisted of one bowl of cereal with watered-down milk; you didn't dare ask for seconds. Lunch was a sandwich and nothing more. At school, after the lunch bell rang, I rummaged through the garbage cans looking for discarded food. When children are hungry, they have no pride, and I was no exception.

The Kind Old Bakery Man

Every Saturday morning, a bakery truck drove down our street ringing a bell. The driver was an elderly man with silver hair and a pleasant smile. He kept the side doors of his truck opened so the aroma of warm bread, donuts and other tasty treats filled the air. When I heard his bell, I would run out and stand by the edge of the street, watching as people flocked to the truck to buy his baked goods. I whimpered as I observed the other kids eating donuts and cookies.

One day as I stood in my usual spot, the truck pulled over to me and stopped.

"Hello there, young lady," the driver said with a great big smile.

I peeked inside his truck; the shelves were full of baked goods.

"Would you like a donut?" he asked.

I could hardly believe my ears. "Yes," I answered breathlessly.

The kind old man reached in, took one off the shelf and handed it to me. It was still warm.

"Here you go, honey, no charge. Just wanted to make a little girl smile today."

He got back behind the wheel of his truck and drove off ringing his bell.

I took two big bites of my jelly donut and ran in the house to show my mother. When I told her about the bakery man giving me a free donut, she got mad. She knew it was because the man felt sorry for me standing at the side of the road. She snatched the half-eaten donut out of my hand, tossed it in the garbage can, and snapped, "No kid of mine is going to embarrass me by getting a handout."

The Breaking of a Habit

My dear mother decided it was time to break me of this "bad habit!" She had a plan. It was cruel and heartless, but fortunately for her, it worked.

One morning when the familiar bells were heard on the street, Mom walked out and approached the truck. She bought two-dozen jelly donuts. When she brought them into the house, I was overwhelmed with excitement. Wow, we were getting jelly donuts after dinner for dessert! Guess she had come into some extra money.

At the dinner table that night, I ate as fast as I could. When finished, I asked Mom if I could have my donut. She went over to the cupboard and brought the two-dozen donuts to the table. She placed them in front of me and commanded me to eat until they were gone. My brothers and sisters looked up from their dinner plates dumbfounded. Was I going to get to eat their donuts too?

At first, I was elated. *Hey, a whole plate of donuts! Wow!* As I was eating, I noticed a belt across my mother's lap. I was beginning to wonder if this was going to be a treat or some sort of punishment for embarrassing her. After about eight or nine donuts, I started to feel nauseous.

"Keep eating, Carol," she commanded.

I tried to obey, but I was starting to feel vomit come up in my throat and into my mouth. I ran from the table, puking donuts all the way to the bathroom. I sat beside the toilet for several hours; the taste of jelly in my mouth made me feel even sicker. When I finally stopped puking, I was instructed to go to bed.

That night I heard her and Dad discussing it.

Mom was angry. "Tom, she embarrasses me, standing by

the street like a starved cat. The neighbors must think we are a welfare case."

"Yes, I suppose you broke her of that today. She ate almost a dozen of those donuts. Doubt she will ever stand by the street again," he replied.

Dad was right; I never did again. Actually, the sound of the bakery bell made me feel sick.

My Fondest Memories, Grandma Bertha

The fondest memories of my childhood were the trips we took every summer to see my dad's family in North Carolina. Dad had two weeks' vacation and he never missed going to see his parents. There were seven of us and the car would only fit three or four at the most. It was up to Mom who got to go and who stayed behind with a relative. Surprisingly enough, I was making the trip almost every year.

The ride to North Carolina was long and the car was cramped, but we all knew the fun that awaited us with our grandparents. Most often, we arrived late in the day, just before bedtime. We took warm baths and then crawled into big comfortable beds.

Grandma patted the tops of our heads when she came in to say goodnight and reminded us to say a prayer before we went to sleep. "See you kids in the morning," she whispered as she left, closing the door behind her.

My sisters and I giggled and poked each other. Then I would snuggle deep under the crisp clean sheets and fall asleep dreaming about the days ahead.

At dawn, the rooster crowed; we woke to the sun peeking through the white lace curtains, casting its warm light into the room. I could smell the bacon and eggs frying in the skillet. I dressed as fast as I could and ran out into the kitchen, where I was greeted by Grandma Bertha's big green eyes and warm smile.

"Good morning, Carol. Did you sleep well?" she inquired as she glided around the kitchen, preparing a big breakfast.

"Oh yes, Grandma Bertha, I slept wonderful."

Grits were boiling on the stove and biscuits were baking in the oven. The milk was fresh from the cow and the fruit was fresh off the tree. I could hardly contain my joy as we gathered around the table to pray blessings on the food.

After breakfast, I wandered around the farm, helping Grandpa feed the livestock and riding on his John Deere tractor.

Grandma Bertha's house was a short distance from the beach. I spent many afternoons on the sandy beach, splashing in the cool Atlantic Ocean. I loved collecting the white seashells. I put them in my bag and took them to show Grandma Bertha. She had seen all sorts of shells, but still she made a fuss over mine. "Oh, those are so pretty, Carol! I bet you found the best ones!"

Peaceful Evenings

Dinner was always wonderful and plentiful at Grandma's house. My dad and his brothers would be out on the water all day. They returned with a fresh catch of shrimp, oysters and clams. A fire was built and grates were placed over the top of it. Then the seafood was piled on the grates. As it steamed, the clamshells opened, the shrimp turned pink and the oysters were ready to be shucked. Hush puppies made of cornmeal, eggs and milk were dropped into hot grease. When they floated to the top, they were plucked out and smeared with fresh butter. The oysters were slimy, so if you had a weak stomach, the sight of one raw could make you queasy. (Me, I loved them, and ate a bunch.) Corn bread, fresh vegetables and cola topped off the meal.

In the evening, the stars filled the sky like a roof of sparkling lights. I lay on the cool ground and watched them twinkle. The moon hung suspended like a mammoth disk. Often, I fell into a peaceful sleep on the front porch as I listened to the crickets and other creatures of the night.

Then in a flash, the two weeks were over.

When the car was packed and we were ready to leave, Grandma Bertha stood outside of the house and gave each one of us a special hug. I always made sure I was last because I wanted to hug her the longest.

You Make Your Grandmother Sick

One year as we packed the car to leave, I sensed Mom was irritated with me. She hid it from Grandma Bertha. Still, I could feel her anger and besides, I knew that look. What could I have done wrong? I was always on my best behavior while we were there.

When it was time to say goodbye, I wrapped my arms around my grandmother's waist and held her tight. She pulled me away gently and gazed into my eyes.

"Child, don't be sad, you will be here next year. I will miss you too. You run along now."

Dad started down the dirt road for the highway, blowing the horn. Everyone waved. I looked out the back window and watched Grandma Bertha until we were out of sight.

Suddenly, I felt a slap across my back; it stung like fire.

I turned and got another blow to my face. My lip burst open.

It was my mother—she was furious! "You make your grandmother sick!" she shouted.

I tried to get away, but there was nowhere in the back seat to escape her wrath. The other kids were ducking. Mom was yelling and swinging at the same time.

"You slob, Grandma Bertha told me that you put your fingers in your nose, then in your mouth. She said you made her sick! You won't be going to North Carolina next year or any year after that!"

My father tried to calm her down. "Dorothy, come on now, my mother didn't say that Carol made her sick; she just commented about her picking her nose, that's all."

Mom was fuming. "That's all? Let me tell you something, Tom. Carol has all sorts of strange habits, like licking her lips and making stupid faces. I have slapped her when she does it, but she still keeps it up."

Dad reached over and touched her knee. "Honey, kids do stuff like that. Carol will grow out of it, relax."

Mom turned back around in her seat.

I crouched on the floorboard, shaking. My brother Ron gave me a sympathetic look. I was bruised and my lip was bleeding.

As we drove the long hours home, I sat in the back seat crying as quietly as possible, scared that my mother would hear me. I could handle the pain of the blows on my back and face; I was sure my habits embarrassed my mother. What was most painful though, was the thought that I could make Grandma Bertha sick! How I wanted to jump out of the car and run back to her loving arms, bury my head in her warm bosom, and promise her that I would never pick my nose again!

Leave Carol Behind

The following year when plans were underway to go to Grandma's, I waited for the verdict. Would I be going or would I be left behind?

For weeks, I had prepared a little speech that I planned to make when I saw Grandma Bertha. I was going to tell her how sorry I was, and that I would not pick my nose and would keep my hands clean.

However, my plans were shattered. I was informed that I would not be making the trip; instead, I would be staying at my aunt's house. The die was cast; there was no changing my mother's mind and I knew better than to try.

The following year, I was left again. The nose-picking incident cemented my mother's decision; I would not be an embarrassment to her. And though Grandma Bertha asked about my absence and requested I be brought down the following year, things remained the same.

Bed-Wetting

I became a chronic bed-wetter in response to the emotional trauma that I endured. I woke up at night drenched in urine and reeking of a foul odor. At eleven years old, I was still struggling with this problem. I tried to mask the smell, but the soaked sheets gave me away.

In order to break me of this, Mom forbade me to have any liquids after six p.m. This became especially difficult during the times that I was sick. I often had high fevers, sometimes topping off at 104 degrees. As the fever raged through my body, I would cry out in the night for water. The more I begged, the more I was refused.

"When you learn to get up and go to the bathroom at

night, then you can have water. Until then, no!"

I went into the bathroom late one night determined to find a way to get some water. I put my mouth on the faucet and turned the knob. However, the water could be heard running through the pipes under the house.

My mother pounded on the bathroom door. "Carol, I am warning you. Don't let me catch you drinking water out of that faucet!"

Drinking Toilet Water

By now, I was frustrated and desperate. I stood there staring at the toilet; there was water in the bowl and it was cold. I got down on my knees next to the commode and lapped up the toilet water. It soothed my dry throat. I continued to do it whenever I was feverish and forbidden a drink.

One night at dinner, I almost passed out. I was running a low-grade fever and my stomach hurt. My skin was a funny yellow color, my eyes the same. I was sent to my room.

It was obvious that I was one sick puppy! I could not get out of bed and my appetite was gone. Mom and Dad were puzzled.

Soon my yellow skin and eyes told the story. I had Hepatitis A. My mother was unaware that I contracted the virus from the toilet water I had been drinking.

However, I was not taken to the doctor; instead, Mom cleared out one of the bedrooms where I would stay until the virus passed. I had to be isolated. She was eight months pregnant and my sister Debbie was only two years old. If this virus spread, she would have a house full of sick kids and that was a risk she was not about to take.

Confined to a Lonely Existence

For over a month, I was banished to a lonely existence. Day after day, I lay on my bed of affliction, too weak to get up.

When I was able to gather up a little strength, I would make my way to the bedroom window. Outside, the kids in the neighborhood were running and playing in the streets. Lonely and sad, I crawled back into my bed and slept for days.

One night the fever woke me. My stomach hurt and my head felt like it was being squeezed in a vise grip. I opened my eyes; the room was very dark. A cool washcloth was pressed on my forehead. At first I thought I might be dreaming. I blinked my eyes to get a closer look. There, sitting on the bed beside me, was my mother. She had come in to try to cool me down with ice water.

"Mom?" I whispered through parched lips.

There was no response. I fell back to sleep.

My older sister Joanne brought in my daily meals. She was always pleasant and sweet to me.

"How are you feeling, Carol?" she asked as she set my food on the table beside the bed.

"I feel terrible, Joanne. My stomach hurts, my bones ache, and I'm nauseated all the time."

She tried to comfort me. "You need to try to eat; it will help you get better."

When she got up to leave, I grabbed her arm. "Joanne, can't you stay with me for a little while?"

She shook her head. "No, what you have is highly contagious; besides, I have a ton of work to do."

At times, the loneliness was unbearable. When I came out to use the bathroom, I would peek around the corner to where the kids were gathered in front of the television watching a game show or a Disney movie. I missed being with my brothers and sisters and I wondered if they missed me as well.

Longing for My Mother's Touch

Once a week, my mother opened the bedroom door and told me to get in the bathtub. There was a cool bath drawn and I was to sit in it for at least a half hour. After I had soaked for a while, Mom would come in and sit down on the side of the tub to wash my hair. Pregnant with my brother Michael, her stomach was very swollen—it looked like it was ready to pop—and she had to balance herself on the side of the tub as best she could. I loved the feeling of her hands in my hair as she lathered the shampoo and then poured the warm water over my head to rinse it out. I always sat very still and said nothing, unless, of course, she asked me a question.

When my bath was finished, she closely checked my body and eyes. Yellow jaundice is a symptom of hepatitis. The whites of your eyes turn yellow, and your skin develops a yellow tint. I guess she had some notion that if the yellow was gone, I was getting better.

As I stood there being examined, I took in her features. To me, my mother was beautiful. She had big brown eyes with thick long lashes. Her skin was like porcelain and she had great cheekbones. And though she was very pregnant, I was impressed with how well she took care of herself. Her nails were manicured and painted, and she always fixed her hair and dressed nicely.

When she was finished inspecting me, I was sent back to the bedroom and told to rest. After I climbed back into my bed, I lay there going over the last hour I had spent with my mother. I longed to lay my head on her breast and express my love for her. I wanted my mother to know that even though she was mad at me most of the time, I loved her anyway.

The "Other Me" Emerges

As I lay sick in bed, I found that strange things occurred.

One night, I was startled by the sound of someone talking in the room. I sat up and looked around—I was alone. I got up, crept over to the window and peered out—there was no one out there either. I crawled back into the bed. Again, I woke up to the same sounds. I knew no one was up and the television was not on.

So who was doing the talking?

I was shocked when I finally realized the "voice" was mine. Words were coming out of my mouth, yet I was making no conscious effort to speak. This totally freaked me out! It was as though someone was inside of my head and using my voice to talk.

"Who are you?" I asked.

"My name is Beth," she answered, "I am you, but a different part of you."

I was stupefied. *How can there possibly be two of me?*

The next night I called out her name in the darkened room. I got a strange sensation, as if someone or something was inside my head. Then I heard her speak.

"That woman you call your mother, she is despicable! Why don't you hate her, Carol? She loathes you and regrets the day you were born!"

I responded, "She doesn't hate me, Beth. Why are you saying such cruel things?"

"They are not cruel; they are true. I am the one who sees things clearly. You are so weak and pathetic."

This is too weird! I have someone else living inside of me and talking with my voice? How can that be? I must be insane. These things do not happen to "normal" people.

Every night after that, Beth emerged. She was angry, cruel and insulting, and she ruthlessly attacked my mother and our relationship. I tried to block her out, but she was strong.

"Cut your wrists; that ought to get that woman's attention." Then she recanted, "Oh forget it; your mother would only be glad to be rid of you!"

I put the pillow over my head and stuck my fingers in my ears.

One evening, exasperated by the battle to silence her, I blurted out, "I have lost my mind!"

Beth responded, "You haven't lost your mind, Carol; I have just taken a piece of it."

Is she right? In my isolation, has my mind splintered off and formed this personality? Is Beth a part of me, a dark evil person that is hidden inside of me and who despises my mother?

For weeks, she prevailed, taunting and ridiculing me.

One night as the battle raged between us, I began pulling out my hair. I scratched my face and banged my head against the wall. I could hear Beth laughing inside my head.

"Go ahead, hurt yourself, Carol; you know it feels good. Go ahead and do it!"

Then, as suddenly as she appeared, she was gone. I was

relieved, but years later, she would return—with a vengeance.

The Road Back to Health

Four long weeks had passed. My plates were going back to the kitchen empty. My appetite had returned and I wasn't fatigued anymore.

One evening my mother entered the room. The sight of her made my heart flutter. She was eight months pregnant when I contracted the hepatitis, and now, a month later, she was ready to give birth.

"It looks like you're feeling better and starting to eat normally again," she said, looking around the stuffy room.

"Yes, Mom, that's true."

She looked closely at me. "The whites of your eyes are clear and your skin has returned to its natural color." She reached over and put her cool hand on my forehead. "It feels like your fever is gone too." She went over and opened the window. "I want this room picked up and I want you to change your bed sheets; I'll send in clean ones. It stinks in here."

When she left the room, the door was open, which meant I could come out and mingle with the rest of the family. I was twelve years old and ready to get back to school and hang out with my friends again.

Two days later, I returned to my normal routine, which consisted of school, a ton of work, cooking, cleaning and taking care of my younger brothers and sisters. *Wonderful!*

Chapter Five

I Am a Bastard

Carol is Not Mine

I woke to a commotion in the kitchen; it was the middle of the night. My sister and I jumped up and headed down the hallway.

"Dorothy, please just let it go," Dad pleaded.

"*Let it go?* Is that what you want me to do, Tom?" my mother screamed. "You sleep around and you just want me to *let it go*?"

It was obvious they were both drunk. She was breaking beer bottles against the wall and glass was flying everywhere.

"You've never been faithful to me, Tom, never!"

Dad fired back at her, "Oh, as if you're so innocent! How about the affair you had with Pat? You know Carol is not mine; she is his kid!"

My mouth dropped opened. My sister Joanne was at my side; she tried to comfort me. "They've been drinking, Carol. Don't let what Dad says affect you. He doesn't mean it!"

Mom was taking things out of the cabinets and throwing them across the room.

Lights in the neighborhood started to go on. People

were standing on their porches pointing at our house and whispering, "The crazy Thompsons are at it again!"

The Police are Here, Again!

The officers were pounding on the front door. It was the same two cops who had been to the house the week before and they didn't look happy about having to come back.

"Okay, folks, we've had several calls at the station; you're disturbing the peace."

My mother went into a rage. "That no good #### kicked me, so I beat him up!"

"Looks like you have been drinking pretty heavy tonight, Mrs. Thompson."

"Mind your own business," she snipped.

The kids and I were huddled in the hallway, crying.

"Have you bothered to think about your children and what this is doing to them?" the cop asked her.

"How dare you talk to me about my kids!" she screamed in his face.

The cop pointed toward the door. "Come on, Mr. Thompson; let's take a ride. Your children need to go back to bed, and so do your neighbors!" They escorted Dad out of the house. They were only intending to keep him long enough for my mother to calm down.

"Yeah, get him out of here! He needs to go to jail." she yelled.

The cop turned and faced her. "Mrs. Thompson, you're the one who should be jailed tonight. You are drunk and disorderly, and your kids are scared to death! You've woken up the entire neighborhood, and personally, I am sick of your big mouth!"

Before the man got out the door, she slammed it shut, just missing his finger. She turned and surveyed the room. There were broken beer bottles and dishes strewn about. We stood there staring at her.

"What the hell are you looking at? Put the baby back to bed and get out here and clean up this mess!" She staggered down the hall to her room and fell into the bed, where she remained until the next day.

The house looked like a bomb hit it. I got a broom and started sweeping up all the broken glass. I felt a stinging on the bottom of my foot; there was blood seeping out. When I examined it, I found a piece of the shard glass. I took a deep breath and yanked it out. Ouch!

I rubbed my eyes and let out a yawn. "It's going to be a long night."

"Long *night*?" my brother moaned as he washed the bloodstains off the walls, "You mean a long *day*; it's already morning!"

The Cup of Poison

Dad's comment about me not being his played in my head over and over again. I tried to forget about it, and for a while, I did—until the night that I was given "the cup of poison."

I was shaken out of a deep sleep; it was Dad.

"Wake up, get your sister Debbie and come in the kitchen."

I climbed out of bed and got my little sister, who was only four.

"Come on," I said, pulling her up and out of the bed, "Dad wants us in the kitchen."

Debbie whimpered, "No, I want to stay in bed."

"Just for a minute; we'll come right back." I took hold of her hand and led her into the brightly lit kitchen.

Being woken up in the middle of the night after they had been drinking was not uncommon. However, this night, I could feel something in the atmosphere, something that had to do with me.

In the kitchen, Mom and Dad were engaged in an intense argument. They both reeked of alcohol.

"You are no better than me," Dad sneered. "She isn't mine and you know it!"

There was a cup on the sink; it had something in it. He picked it up and asked my mother, "Who should I give it to?"

"Give it to Carol," my mother told him. "She's the one you question, right?"

I looked up at my parents and said, "I don't want a drink. I'm not thirsty."

Drink It!

Dad shoved the cup toward me. "Drink it!" he demanded.

Debbie was tired and cranky; she was pulling on my arm and whining, "I want to go back to bed!"

I tried to calm her as they continued to argue and push each other around the kitchen.

"Go ahead, Carol, drink it," Dad commanded.

I took the cup; the contents had a strong odor. As the liquid touched my lips, it stung. Then I realized what it was ... bleach! The cup had bleach in it and I was being forced to drink it. I obeyed and took a sip. I winced from the horrible taste.

Suddenly I felt an impact; the cup went sailing across the kitchen.

"Are you crazy, Tom? You would poison your own daughter?"

His answer would haunt me for years to come: "She may be your daughter, Dorothy, but she sure isn't mine. She's a bastard and you know it; she came out of your whoring around!"

My mother went into a rage; she dragged her nails down his face. "I'm no whore! The women you've been bedding since I married you, they're the whores!"

I took Debbie by the hand and took her back to bed. I slipped beneath the covers and pulled her close to me. She whimpered then fell asleep. Throughout the night, until the sun came up the next morning, my father's words kept replaying in my head. *She is not mine!*

Beaten Like a Dog

One afternoon, about a week after the "poison cup" incident, I was outside in the yard with my younger brother. An argument broke out between us; it was over something trivial. Dad heard us arguing and came outside.

"Carol, stop irritating him."

"It's not me, Dad, it's him. He started it," I said, pointing at my brother.

Dad's voice was stern. "Carol, get down in the basement."

"But, I didn't do anything," I protested.

As we headed down the stairs, I heard him pulling the belt out of the loops on his pants. Then he folded it in half. When I turned to face him, he had a crazed look.

He started swinging it wildly. It caught my cheek, neck and back. When I ran, he chased me and continued the beating. I was covered in wounds and welts. I kept begging him to stop and promising that I would not fight with my brother anymore. I fell to the floor. As I crawled away, I felt the final wrath of his belt across my back. My shirt was stained with blood. I went into a corner and crouched like a beaten dog.

Then he stopped, as if he had come out of a trance. Without a word, he went up the stairs.

That night there was no supper for me.

Dad's Mental Illness

Things were going from bad to worse. Dad's kidneys were infected; he had liver problems and his blood pressure was out of control. He was hospitalized and had to have surgery.

According to my mother, something happened to him after he received the anesthetic. She was convinced that either the doctors gave him too much, or he was having a bad reaction to it. Shortly after the operation, before Dad had fully recovered, he signed himself out of the hospital and arrived home in a cab, wearing his pajamas. Mom was shocked when he walked into the house.

"What are you doing here and where are your clothes, Tom?"

He told her that he had been released from the hospital, and they had lost his clothes.

The next day, Mom went storming into the hospital. When she finished reaming everyone there, the doctor in charge sat her down in his office and explained.

"Mrs. Thompson, your husband's mental condition has nothing to do with the operation or the medicine we used."

Mom stood up and towered over his desk. "Now, you listen to me, Doctor, my husband has been acting wacky since he came out from under that anesthetic." She left in a huff, promising she would sue "the pants off of them!"

Nothing ever came of Mom's accusations against the hospital. Nevertheless, I can tell you this, Dad was never the same—never!

When the flourmill where Dad was employed found out that he was sick, they considered him a risk and let him go. He was devastated! He gradually fell into a state of severe depression and began to do strange things.

He plastered notes on all the doors of the house with scribbled warnings, that if the doorknobs were turned, the house would explode. I came home from school one day to find a note on the front door that read, "Crawl through the basement window to get in, there are booby traps everywhere." As the madness progressed, he told the neighbors that the house was being watched by the FBI and there were top-secret files hidden in the attic.

As for my mother, she got herself a boyfriend, and so many nights she stayed gone until morning. Guess she was catching up on all the years she was pregnant and out of shape.

The House is on Fire

One night, I woke to a stinging sensation in my throat. When I opened my eyes, there was smoke everywhere. I jumped out of my bed and went into the living room, where I discovered Dad asleep on the couch. A lit cigarette had fallen from his mouth and was burning a deep hole in the couch.

The kids were crying from their beds because of the smoke; it was choking them and burning their eyes. Despite the fact that it was snowing outside and very cold, I knew I had to get them out of the house. I rustled them out of the beds and grabbed the baby out of the crib. My sister and I were heading for the back door when my father came up off the couch. He staggered toward me with his hand raised; I covered my face. He swung and missed me.

"What the hell are you trying to do?" he yelled.

"Dad, the house is full of smoke! The kids are choking; I am trying to get them to fresh air."

"Is your mother home?" he asked.

"No, Dad," I answered.

I could see the anger in his face. He had mixed his tranquilizers with alcohol—a deadly brew—and he could barely stand up. The man was clearly out of his senses.

"Take the kids downstairs and sit close to the furnace," he ordered me.

I picked up my baby brother and led the kids down to the dark basement. We huddled around the furnace on the concrete floor; it was ice cold. The kids were whimpering and complaining. They were frightened and wanted to go back to bed. I could hear Dad moving around upstairs. I noticed that the smoke was increasing. *What is he doing?*

Then I heard the sirens. There was shuffling upstairs, voices and the sound of a window breaking. Suddenly, the basement was flooded with a bright light. I heard a voice exclaim, "Oh my God, there are kids down here!" It was a fireman. He was shining his flashlight at us.

The neighbors took us into their homes until the smoke

cleared and the fire was put out. We were told that Dad had started the other couch on fire. He told the police that his wife had been out all night with another man, and that he was angry so he was going to ruin her furniture.

Mom showed up the next day. Her living room had two charred couches, a broken window from where they released some of the smoke out of the house, and black walls.

That day she and Dad fought like animals.

"You are a whore!" Dad shouted, "Gone all night with another man!"

"I am catching up for the years you ran around on me with other women, Tom!" she shouted back at him.

Total Mayhem

Two days later, Dad attempted to hang himself. The rig broke and he fell to the floor. He showed Mom the rope burns around his neck.

Things were getting hairy and Mom was beginning to worry about her husband's behavior. No one was safe. Then, to make matters worse, she woke up in the middle of the night to find him kneeling over her with a pillow in his hands.

"If I can't have you, no one else will," he hissed as he pressed the pillow against her face.

In terror, she fought him until she was able to push him off.

The next morning, Dad sat at the kitchen table and cried. "What's wrong with me, Dorothy? Why am I doing these terrible things? I can't seem to help myself ..."

My mother knew it was time to get help for her husband, before he hurt her, himself or the kids. Shortly after, he was admitted into a mental institution, eighty miles away.

The day he left, he cried like a baby. "I will be good, honey. Don't let them take me, please!"

I sat on my bed listening as he begged her to let him stay home.

Mom tried to reason with him. "They can help you, Tom, and you will be home in a few months."

"But, honey, I want to stay here with you and the kids!"

A Broken Man

I watched out the window as Mom walked Dad to the car that would take him to the hospital. At that moment, my mind was flooded with the memories of when, years before, they had taken away my little brother Cronley. I was in agony trying to digest all the pain. I knew deep inside that Dad was not a bad man. He loved his family. Sure, he had a wandering eye, but he loved his wife, and deep down she knew that. He had worked hard at his job at the flourmill. When they let him go, they gave him the shaft, and it tore him up to think he would not able to support his family anymore. Besides, he was sick all the time, suffering from high blood pressure, kidney disease, liver problems, emotional distress and depression.

I was divided about the feelings I had for him. They were both bitterness and brokenness; bitterness because of the times he hurt me, and brokenness because, in spite of his faults, he was the only father I knew. At that very minute, I was overwhelmed with pity for him.

I watched as the car disappeared around the corner. The image of his face haunted me. It was the look of a lost little boy, with a tear-streaked face, being taken away from the only thing he ever loved ... his family!

CHAPTER SIX

A Safe Port in the Storm

The Meeting

*W*hen I was thirteen years old, I met a girl named Marilyn. She was pretty, popular, and every guy at school wanted to date her, while every girl wanted to be her "BFF." I was convinced that someone as cool as Marilyn would not give me the time of day. Why would she want to associate with "trash" like me?

Marilyn lived on Hedley Street, just one block over from us, in a tall three-story house. Whenever Mom sent me to the store, I made it a point to pass by, in hopes that she would be outside on the porch. One Sunday afternoon as I moseyed on by, I spotted her sitting there with a big old tomcat on her lap. She was stroking his fur and talking to him. She looked up, saw me walking by and smiled. I smiled back.

"Hey, aren't you Carol Thompson?"

"Yes, I am."

"I thought so. I see you pass by here a lot. Why don't you sit with me for a while?"

I could hardly catch my breath! *Marilyn wants to sit and talk to me? Wow!*

I knew my mother would have a cow if I were gone too long. However, this was one of the most popular girls in school and I was not about to let this opportunity pass me by. I sat down with her. We started chatting about our classes, the teachers we loathed, cute guys and movie stars.

"Well, I better get going. I was on my way to the store for my mother," I told her as I got up to leave.

"Hey, want to come over tomorrow after school?" she asked.

"Sure," I sputtered.

As I hurried along to the store, I was bubbling inside. Marilyn wanted me to come over to her house and hang out, imagine that!

The next day after school, when I had finished doing all my chores, I rushed over to Marilyn's house. Her mother let me in and directed me to Marilyn's bedroom. When I entered, she was standing in front of the mirror fixing her gorgeous auburn hair. I had to admit, I was intimidated at the sight of her. To begin with, Marilyn was pretty and very well developed for her age. I looked down at my shabby clothes and blushed with embarrassment, but her sweetness put me at ease. That day was the beginning of a friendship that would change my life.

An Unfamiliar Kindness

We were two typical thirteen-year-olds; we spent our time yapping on the phone, gossiping about people, getting into trouble and just having fun.

One day as I was leaving her house, she stopped me at the door. In her hand was a hanger; on it was a blouse and skirt.

"Here, Carol, these colors will look great on you. Why don't you wear this to school tomorrow?"

"Do you think I am a charity case, Marilyn?"

"Absolutely not, if I want to share my clothes with you, what is the big deal? Just take them!" She pushed the clothes at me. "Go ahead, I insist, take them."

So I did. The next morning, I was shaking with excitement as I dressed for school. Marilyn was right; the clothes did look nice on me. As I was walking out the door to catch the bus, my mother intercepted me.

"What are you wearing?" she asked, looking me up-and-down.

"Nothing," I responded.

"Don't tell me 'nothing'!" she snapped. "Now, where did you get those clothes?"

I explained to her that my new friend Marilyn let me borrow them.

"You are not a welfare case. Give them back and wear your own clothes."

I said that I would, but I didn't, and the next time Marilyn lent me something cool to wear (and she did every week), I changed in the bathroom at school.

The Hand that Feeds Me

It was lunchtime in the cafeteria. Marilyn handed me a bag.

"What's this?" I asked.

She smiled sweetly and replied, "Your lunch; go ahead, open it. I made it myself."

I dug inside and pulled out the contents. There was a ham sandwich, a banana, homemade chocolate chip cookies, and to top it off, a can of Pepsi. Overcome with emotion, I asked, "Why did you do this for me?"

"Because you're my best friend, Carol, and you need to have a nice lunch. I don't like seeing you go without."

Marilyn was always looking out for me. She was thoughtful and caring, and she took a genuine interest in my wellbeing. If people mocked me, Marilyn defended me. When someone pushed me around, she fought for me.

I made a promise to myself that one day I would pay her back for all she had done for me. When I told her about it, she laughed.

"You don't owe me anything, Carol. This is what friendship is all about, right? I look out for you, and you look out for me; one hand washes the other."

Marilyn was a godsend. She was at my house almost every day after school to help me with the kids and my chores. The workload was overwhelming, but Marilyn being there made it fun and easy. We all loved her. Sometimes she would bring over ingredients to make cookies and cakes. She ironed, washed clothes, and helped me make meals. I knew it meant missing football games and school activities, but she never complained. The girl was amazing. Surprisingly, Mom really liked her. Listen, if my mother genuinely liked someone, it showed, and Marilyn won her over quickly; she called her "Aunt Dorothy."

The Molestation

Marilyn was a port in the storm. A person who was more than a friend, she was a confidant. I was safe with her and I could tell her anything. One day I confessed something that I had not told a living soul. It was something I had hidden deep down inside and now wanted to get off my chest.

It was a cold autumn day. We were huddled under a blanket in her garage, drinking beer that Marilyn had sneaked out of the house.

"Marilyn, if I tell you a secret, do you swear you won't tell anyone?"

She was quick to remind me that I was her best friend and that she would never repeat anything. I got out from under the blanket, walked over to the garage door and looked out to see if anyone was around. The coast was clear. I went back and sat down, and then I unloaded something that was eating me up inside for a long time.

"Well, Marilyn, it happened when I was eight. A man that I knew took me down into his basement; he told me he was going to give me money to buy ice cream. I wanted the ice cream pretty badly, so I went with him. When we got down there, he told me he wanted to do something before he gave me the money, but that I was to tell no one or I would get in big trouble ..."

I was too embarrassed to finish.

"Go on, Carol, you can tell me what happened; take your time," Marilyn said as she stroked my arm.

I Tell it All

"Well, Marilyn, he started touching me, you know what I mean?"

"Yes," she replied.

"When I protested, he tried to soothe me by saying that it was okay and that he liked me. He told me that a lot of people did this, but they didn't admit it. When he was done, he gave me the money and I bought the ice cream. I promised myself I would never let him do that to me again. But he convinced me that it was too late, I had already let him, what did it matter?"

I glanced up to see her reaction. There was compassion in her eyes.

"I felt so dirty, Marilyn. I would go into the bathroom and put a washcloth under scolding hot water and rub it across my stomach to burn away the feeling of shame."

Marilyn put her arm around my shoulder to comfort me.

"He said I liked it and asked for it, but that's not true, Marilyn, I didn't!"

"Did he go inside of you, Carol?"

"No," I answered quickly, "never! But it was ugly and I hated it!"

"Do your parents know about this?" she asked.

"No."

We sat there for a few minutes, neither of us talking. Marilyn was trying to process what I had just revealed to her. I could see that it bothered her a lot.

Then she turned to me and said, "Carol, I will make sure no one ever hurts you again! When we are eighteen, you will move away from all that craziness and we will get an apartment together. We will travel across the country and have a wonderful time. And all these terrible things that you have had to go through will soon be forgotten, I promise!"

That night, as I walked down the street toward home, the cold wind howled through the trees. Above me, thick clouds blocked out the light of the moon. There was darkness all around. I thought about what Marilyn had promised me about our future and I smiled. In spite of the dark night, her promises made me feel lit up and warm inside.

Louie, My First Love

I was born in November; Marilyn, in October. The year we turned sixteen, we were drinking, acting wild, and "boy crazy." Mikki, who lived across the street from me, started hanging out with us. We called ourselves the "terrible trio."

One night while standing around on a street corner, looking for someone of age to buy us beer, a hot-looking red car pulled up. Someone called out, "Hey girls, want to go for a ride?"

I walked over and peered inside the car. I recognized Louie Page, who was sitting in the front seat. "Will you guys buy us some beer?" I asked boldly.

"Sure, climb in."

We rode around for hours, listening to music, telling crude jokes and drinking. Louie and I landed up in the back seat, kissing. By the time they dropped us off, my lips were chapped. Marilyn ribbed me about it.

"Hey, your lips are all red. Is he a good kisser?"

I giggled, "Yes, he is awesome."

After that night, Louie started calling me every day. It was hard to stay on the phone because my mother was so strict. At school, we sat together at lunch and strolled down the hallways, holding hands. Within a month, we were an item and inseparable.

Innocence Lost to a Thing Called "Love"

About six months into our "steady relationship," Louie and I started experimenting with sex. First baby steps, then it graduated to some serious messing around. One night, in a fit of passion, I lost my virginity to him on the living room floor. It was quick and uneventful. It hurt and I was ashamed. Louie took off right after it happened and did not call me for days, which really hurt.

I cried non-stop. When I saw him at school, he avoided me. I was falling apart and my emotions were getting out of control. I became depressed and considered suicide. I had pains in my chest during the day and cried myself to sleep at night.

Finally, one afternoon Louie showed up at my locker.

"I miss you" was all he said.

We met behind the school that night. As soon as we wandered away from the crowd, we were having sex again. I felt guilty, but I wanted to hold onto Louie and was sure I could keep him close if he and I were lovers.

With this new thing called "love," I found myself dealing with all kinds of emotions: passion, jealousy, confusion, anger and lust. One minute, we were locked in each other's arms, proclaiming our undying love. The next, we were arguing and threatening to break-up. I was possessive and he was jealous. At times, I wanted him all to myself; and then, for no reason, I wanted him out of my life. It was like a wild roller coaster ride, filled with ups, downs and sharp curves.

"Are You and Louie Doing It?"

While riding the bus to school one day, Marilyn asked me, "Are you and Louie doing it?"

I was quiet.

"You are, aren't you? Tell me, what is it like?"

"It's okay, I guess."

"Carol, we are best friends and you tell me everything. Now tell me, how is it?"

I was nervous. "Well, it makes me feel bad afterward."

Now it was my turn to ask the question. "Are you and Joey messing around?"

She giggled, "A little, but not really. He is so shy."

"Well, be glad you're not, because I regret that Louie and I did it so soon."

Marilyn looked surprised. "Really?"

"Marilyn, it has made me crazy. Do yourself a favor and wait before you and Joey do it."

CHAPTER SEVEN

A Closer Look at Dorothy

Could This Be the Reason for Her Hard Heart?

I often wondered what made my mother such a cold woman! There was an obvious struggle that took place inside her when it came to expressing love, especially for her children. I can honestly say that there was not one time that she held me, touched me affectionately, or ever said, "I love you." Never!

There were days when she seemed melancholy, and when in these moods, she would open up about her childhood. She told me about something that happened to her when she was nine years old—something that I have always believed had a significant impact on her life and her behavior.

When Dorothy's mother (my grandmother) was sixteen years old, she was molested by an older man who lived in the neighborhood. His family had a successful business and they were respected in the community. After repeatedly taking advantage of the young girl, she became pregnant with Dorothy. When the young man was confronted, he denied it and his family stood behind him.

Dorothy was born without a father. Her young mother was shunned and ridiculed for accusing a prominent family's son for her predicament. When Dorothy was one year old, her mother met and married a man fifteen years older than her. He gave the child his name and later fathered three other children with his wife. Dorothy was unaware that he was not her biological father.

"I noticed that he was more affectionate with the other kids and was much stricter with me," she told me, "but, all in all, he was good to me."

A Shocking Revelation

One day Dorothy and her aunt walked into the grocery store to purchase some cold cuts. The man behind the counter looked closely at the young girl and asked her name.

After they left the store, her aunt asked her, "Dorothy, do you know who that man behind the counter was?"

"No, Auntie, I do not," she answered.

"That, my dear, was your father."

Dorothy was confused. "No, my father is at home."

"The man at home is your stepfather; he married your mother after you were born and gave you his name. Your brother and two sisters are his biological children. However, that man in the store, he is your real father!"

"I wanted to go back and meet him, but Auntie forbade me," my mother told me.

"Did you ever try to find him after that encounter?" I asked curiously.

"No, he took advantage of my mother and denied I was his child, so why should I? It is what it is," she said flippantly, "life goes on and so did I!"

One Tough Broad

Yes, Dorothy was a strong-willed woman. She had a hard life! There were many times that circumstances knocked the feet out from under her. However, she refused to stay down. She pulled herself up by the bootstraps and went on, always ready for the next battle. I admired that about her.

If she said this once, she said it a thousand times: "When you get hurt or slapped down, don't sit around feeling sorry for yourself; it accomplishes nothing! Instead, get up off your sorry a** and get back on your feet; that is what really matters! It's not the hit that you take or how hard you fall, it's the comeback!"

The Revelation

Late one night the phone rang; it jolted me out of a deep sleep. I glanced at the clock; it was three-thirty in the morning. I thought it might be the mental hospital calling to inform us that Dad had escaped again. We often received late-night calls warning us that he had gotten out through a window or an unlocked door and was headed home.

I picked up the phone; it was my mother.

"Get up, get dressed and drive the car here to the Town Shanty Bar. The keys are in my top drawer."

"What about the kids?" I asked.

"They'll be fine; they are all sleeping!" She hung up.

I stood there rubbing the sleep out of my eyes. What did she want, and why was I going out in the middle of the night to a bar?

I slipped into a pair of shorts and a tee shirt, put on my sneakers and grabbed the keys to her car. I headed out the door to the bar that was only five minutes away. I drove slowly and cautiously. A soft, misty rain made the deserted blacktop road look shiny and slick.

When I arrived, there were only two cars in the parking lot. I walked through the front door and looked around the room. Except for the bartender, there was no one else there.

"Excuse me, sir, my mother called me from here."

He nodded and pointed to a back room.

"Thank you," I told him and then walked back in that direction.

The room was noticeably dark. I spotted my mother in the corner; she was locked in an intimate embrace with a man that I did not recognize. They were kissing passionately. When he spotted me, he pulled away.

"Dorothy, I think that's Carol."

She motioned for me to come. I gingerly approached them. Her companion was a tall, handsome man. A look of pride came over my mother's face and then she made the introduction:

"Carol, this is Pat."

I looked into his brown eyes and meekly said, "Hello."

"I have waited a long time to meet you, Carol," he replied in a husky voice.

A Stranger?

Suddenly the bartender appeared, interrupting the moment. "Hey, I am ready to lock up, folks."

As we walked out to the parking lot, I noticed Pat was studying me closely.

"How old are you, Carol?" he inquired.

"I'm sixteen," I replied without looking at him.

He placed his hand on my shoulder. "You were two

years old the last time I saw you," he said affectionately.

Mom told me to get into the car.

"Goodnight, sir." I held out my hand to shake his.

He took it and squeezed it gently. "Carol, this was nice; I hope we meet again."

I walked over to the driver's side of my mother's car and got in. I observed them through the window as they were saying good-bye. Mom tried to kiss him, but he pulled away.

I heard him protest, "Not now, Dorothy; I'll call you. Goodnight."

My mother got into the car as Pat walked away; he turned, glanced in my direction then got into his car and drove off.

That Man is Your Father

"Who was that man?" I asked. "He said he knew me when I was two years old. Is he a friend of the family?"

Mom laughed aloud. "No, my dear, he is not 'a friend of the family.' When I was in my twenties, I had an affair with him and I think he is your father."

I clutched the steering wheel so tightly that my knuckles turned white. "What are you saying?" I asked in disbelief.

"I am saying that the man you met tonight is your father; is that so hard to understand?"

I dared to ask, "Why, after all these years, are you telling me this now?"

There was no response.

I looked over; she was out cold. The smell of alcohol filled the car. I was disgusted.

When we got to the house, I shook her.

"Mom, come on, you need to go in the house to bed."

She mumbled incoherently, woke up cursing and crawled out of the car. When we got in the house, she fell on the bed. I covered her with a blanket and left the room.

Now the pieces were starting to fit together. Dad knew; that is why he treated me differently. The night he tried to force me to drink the "poison cup," calling me a bastard and denying he was my father, this was the reason.

How ironic, Dorothy had been shocked into hearing that she was a bastard child. Now she had done the same thing to me, her daughter. Was this her revenge? Did she feel justified because it happened to her in the same manner, abruptly and unexpectedly? Did she want me to feel the same "disconnected feeling" that she had?

In bed that night, I pounded my chest with my fists and cried out, "Why?" I felt like my heart was being torn to pieces. Yes, my dad was hard on me, but at least I belonged. I knew we were a dysfunctional family, but still, I belonged. Now, I felt separated from the rest of the kids, like an out-cast. Inside, I felt different.

After that night, I never saw Pat again.

CHAPTER EIGHT

God Takes My Best Friend

"Marilyn, What's Wrong?"

It was a Friday night. We had made plans to go out driving around. Marilyn was supposed to pick Mikki and me up around seven. She was an hour late.

So, rather than call, we decided to walk the short distance to her house. When we arrived, we were surprised to find Marilyn sick and in bed.

"Come on Marilyn, let's go out and have some fun," I urged.

"No, you guys go ahead. My muscles and joints hurt. I can't go out tonight."

Her mother entered the room. "Marilyn isn't going anywhere; she has been sick all day. You girls need to leave."

So we did. We headed to our usual place to meet Louie and our friends. As I sat sipping a cold beer, the image of Marilyn lying in bed, sick and pale, was stuck in my mind. When Louie showed up, I was distracted.

"What's wrong?" he asked, taking a swig from my bottle of beer.

"Marilyn is sick," I told him.

"People get sick all the time; don't be so concerned. She will be fine. Come on, let's go be alone somewhere." He pulled me up off the steps.

"No, Louie, I am just not into it."

He stepped back as if I slapped him. "What is the problem, Carol?"

I tossed my half-empty bottle in the bushes and started walking toward home. He was stunned, but did not attempt to follow me. I passed Marilyn's house and peered up at her bedroom window; it was dark. I assumed she was asleep. I sat down on the cool grass and thought about Louie. I wondered if he was mad at me for taking off. I had explained to him countless times how important Marilyn was to me and how much she had done for me through the years. Surely, he understood …

The next morning, the phone rang; it was seven-thirty.

"Who is calling this house this early in the morning?" my mother yelled from her bed.

"That was Marilyn's mother. Marilyn was rushed to the hospital last night. She is not well and she is asking for me. Can I go and see her, Mom?"

Ordinarily, my mother would have said, "Absolutely not!" But she really liked Marilyn, and I believe she was genuinely concerned, so she let me go.

When I walked into the hospital room, Marilyn was sitting on the bed.

"What is wrong?" I asked.

"My joints are killing me, Carol. My mother brought me here last night and they admitted me. The doctors have ordered a bunch of tests."

I sat beside her on the bed and tried to soothe her fears. She was really shaken up and so was I.

Terminal

A few days later, a team of doctors met with Marilyn's mother to give her the test results. When they told her what they had found, she almost passed out. She decided not to tell Marilyn the severity of her condition. Instead, she told her that it was a blood disorder and it would clear up. The truth was the blood disorder was terminal and Marilyn's days were numbered.

After a few weeks in the hospital, they released Marilyn. The disease posed no immediate threat, and so she was able to finish out the school year. However, they informed her mother that it would come on quickly and when it did, it would progress rapidly.

Marilyn and I were ecstatic that she would be returning to school. We tried to pick up where we had left off, before she had gotten sick. However, Marilyn tired easily, so she had to be careful. Besides, her mother was always doting over her and making sure that she did not over exert herself.

With Graduation Comes Change

I failed my last year of school, so I did not graduate. As for Marilyn, she passed with high honors and attended the senior prom with the best-looking guy in school.

School was out. We were technically done with our education. Most of the graduates were making plans for their future, enjoying their freedom, and going on vacations. Marilyn planned to enroll in some courses at the local college. However, she started feeling sick again. Her joints were swollen and she was in constant pain. She lost her appetite and it was difficult to get her to eat anything, so the doctors insisted she be readmitted into the hospital. Marilyn was crushed.

I spent every minute of the day with her. When visiting hours began in the morning, I was there, bright and early. At night, the nurses had to practically push me out the door. When friends called and invited me to go out, I declined. Marilyn needed me, and I was not about to go out and enjoy activities with others while my friend lay on her back in a hospital.

No Regrets, No Goodbye

I was seventeen years old when I packed my belongings and moved out of my parents house and in with Marilyn's family. My mother made no effort to stop me. I guess she figured it was one less mouth to feed. She was well aware of how sick Marilyn was and she knew I was spending every waking hour with her. The day I was packing to leave, she came into the bedroom.

"So, how is Marilyn?" she asked.

"Sick, real sick," I answered.

She turned around and walked out.

When I was leaving, I called out, "Mom," but there was no answer. I did not want to leave without saying goodbye. Funny, I could not find her anywhere. The car was in the driveway, but she was not around.

I walked out the door and down the street carrying my bags. My heart ached with an all-too-familiar pain, the same one that I felt as a little girl when my mother left me on my first day of school. I wanted to cry, but the tears did not come; I was empty and dry.

My Priority, Marilyn

Most of the time Marilyn was in the hospital, but on some weekends the doctor let her come home. She was under close watch, but being at home helped her feel a whole lot better. We slept in her bed together, just like old times, and watched television for hours on end. Marilyn loved the soaps and the talk shows. When the weather permitted, we went out on the front porch and sat in the sun, soaking up the rays. Her old tomcat would crawl up on her lap; Marilyn stroked his fur and cooed at him. These were the good times. We laughed, and sometimes we were able to forget that she was sick.

As the months passed and the disease progressed, our outdoor activity ceased. Marilyn became paranoid about her appearance. She feared someone might see how thin she was or how much hair she had lost. Her skin cracked and bled, so I rubbed her with moisturizer. This killer disease was sucking the life out of her, and since she was unaware of how sick she was, it was difficult for her to understand why she was not improving.

"When am I going to get better, Carol?" she asked.

I was not sure how to answer her. "Soon, Marilyn, very soon."

She looked puzzled. "But I seem to be getting worse, don't you think?"

Again, I was lost for words. "It takes time, that's all. You will improve, you'll see."

Inside my heart, I knew my dear friend was dying, but I refused to believe it. I could not accept the fact that one day she would not be there.

Late at night, as I lay beside her in the bed at home, I listened closely to her shallow breathing. It was impossible for me to sleep because I lived in constant fear that it might be the last breath she would draw.

A Surprise Call

I was surprised and excited when I got a call from Louie.

"I miss you, Carol. Do you want to go out tonight?"

I was happy and relieved to hear his voice again, but it had been a hard day for Marilyn and I did not want to leave her alone. "No, I can't Louie. Marilyn needs me."

"Do you have to be with her 24/7?" he asked, obviously annoyed. "I understand that she is sick, Carol, but you have a life too!"

"Marilyn is my life, Louie," I told him through clenched teeth, "and don't you ever forget that!"

After that, we did not see each other for over three months. I was aware that he was seeing other girls and I was jealous. However, my devotion to Marilyn was my top priority; it took precedence over any wants or needs of my own.

Marilyn Insists That I Call Louie

Marilyn celebrated her eighteenth birthday in the hospital. She refused a cake, visitors, or any type of festivity. I was the only friend allowed in the room. She was glum and depressed. I was depressed too, but I refused to let her see it.

As we sat staring at the television, she asked me, "What are you thinking about, Carol? You seem so far away. This place is starting to get the best of you, isn't it? Tell me the truth."

"No, I'm okay. I love being here with you, Marilyn. To be honest, I was thinking about Louie. I have not seen him in a long time. I hear he is dating."

"That's because you don't spend any time with him, Carol. You are here all the time. I think you should give him a call."

"He's pretty much gotten on with his life. He's going out with Patty Brenner," I told her.

"Well, it doesn't mean he doesn't miss you."

Marilyn insisted I call him, so I did.

Back in Louie's Arms

I was a nervous wreck as I waited for Louie to answer the phone.

"Hey, Louie, how are you?"

"I'd be a lot better if I could see you," he responded. (Talk about being direct … he made no bones about getting together.)

When I informed Marilyn, she seemed genuinely happy.

"You need to get out of here for a while, Carol; this hospital is such a drag. I can't leave, but you can."

That night, when I was sure Marilyn was comfortable, I left to meet Louie. It was a cold winter night in January. The wind chill was below zero. I shivered as I walked through the parking lot to the car.

Louie and I had made plans to meet at a local bar. When I arrived, he wasn't there. I wondered if maybe he had changed his mind. I ordered a drink and sat down in a booth. After about ten minutes, he walked through the door. The sight of my young love took my breath away. He sat down across from me.

"You look good, Carol, real good."

"So do you, Louie."

We sipped our drinks, staring over the rim of the glass

into each other's eyes.

"How is Marilyn?"

"Not good, Louie. I keep hoping she will feel better, but it is not happening."

"Is she dying, Carol?"

"No, I won't let her," I answered abruptly.

"Carol, do you think you can stop her from dying?"

I didn't answer. I was trying to hold back the tears.

He came over and sat beside me. I laid my head on his shoulder.

Louie stood up, helped me with my coat, and led me out the door to his car. We drove to a hotel without speaking. When we entered the room, I fell into his arms.

"I have missed you, Carol," he whispered, "I can't get you out of my mind."

"Oh, Louie, I think about you all the time."

He sighed, "What are we going to do? Can we get back what seems to be slipping away?"

"I don't know," I answered, "just hold me, Louie, hold me close."

He did.

When I woke the next morning, he was lying there staring at me.

"What time is it? I have to get to the hospital," I said, reaching for my clothes.

"Wait a minute, Carol, just slow down." His expression turned serious. "What about us? Do you want to just call it quits?"

I tried to explain, "My life is very complicated right now, Marilyn being sick and all."

He shook his head in frustration. "I can't do this anymore Carol. We are drifting apart. I understand how devoted you are to Marilyn, but this is ridiculous. Your life is swallowed up in her, and there doesn't seem to be any room left for us anymore!" After having said that, he got up, dressed and left.

Our Love Child

When I missed my period, I did not think much of it. I was sure the stress of Marilyn being ill and my grueling schedule had delayed it. But as it turned out, I was carrying Louie's child.

"Have you told him?" Marilyn asked, expressing excitement at the thought of a baby.

"Not yet."

Before I could tell him the news, he showed up at the hospital. After visiting with Marilyn, he asked me to step into the hallway. As soon as we were alone, he asked me outright, "Are you pregnant?"

I was flabbergasted. "How did you find out?"

"Never mind that; what do you want to do about it, Carol?"

I didn't know what to say. "I need time," I replied. "My mother doesn't even know yet. She is going to have a cow when she finds out."

"Well, I will do the right thing and marry you, if you want," he whispered.

"This is not the time to discuss it," I said as I walked away.

"Are you kidding? This is our life and our kid, so when would you say the right time is?"

"I will call you, I promise." I left him standing there and went back into the hospital room.

Breaking the News to Mom

It was time to inform my mother about the "bundle of joy" that I was carrying.

She looked at me as if I were an alien. "How did you get yourself into that predicament?"

I laughed. "You had ten kids and you're asking me how I got pregnant. I should think you have the answer to that by now, Mom."

She was not amused and resented my sarcasm. "Well, I suppose Louie is the father. Will he marry you?"

"I don't want to marry Louie. It would never work out."

She laughed. "No marriage of yours will ever work out, my dear."

I left the house resenting her more than when I arrived.

I Make My Decision

For weeks, I thought about what to do. I paced the hallway of the hospital. I still had no answers. Therefore, I made a decision—one I would later regret. I decided not to let Louie be a father to this child. I would do it another way, without him. My devotion was to Marilyn and, pregnant or not, I intended to stay by her side.

Naturally, I did not tell Marilyn all the details. I simply informed her that I was taking a different route with the baby. She asked just a few questions.

"What did Louie say?"

"He said he would do the right thing," I answered.

"Do you love him, Carol?" Her tone was serious.

I quickly responded, "Yes, I do, but the love Louie and I share is complex, and I doubt it would make a happy marriage."

Marilyn Takes a Turn for the Worst

I arrived at the hospital one day to find nurses scurrying in and out of Marilyn's room. They made me wait in the hall. She was hooked up to all kinds of machines.

When they left the room, I sat down beside her. "Marilyn, what's wrong?"

"Carol, the pain is unbearable. Help me."

I reached over and touched her hand. "What can I do? Tell me and I will do it."

She had a strange, fearful look on her face. "Carol, I am so scared!" she confessed. A tear trickled down her cheek.

I wiped it with my finger. "Don't be afraid, Marilyn. I'm here."

As the pain intensified, they increased her morphine. The stuff was potent and caused Marilyn to hallucinate. She saw people in the room that were not there. She imagined spiders crawling on her bed. I tried to tell her it was the meds but she insisted that these things were real. So I stopped arguing with her and pretended I saw them too.

I decided to start spending nights at the hospital to be with Marilyn as much as possible. I slept in a lounge chair in her hospital room. When I woke one morning, my friend was weeping.

"What's wrong? Are you in pain? Should I call for a nurse?"

She shook her head. "No. I just want you to know that I appreciate you being here with me all the time—"

I interrupted her, "Marilyn, I love coming and spending time with you. I'm just giving back all that you have given to me through the years."

I stood up to stretch and walked over to the window. Down below on the street, people were going about their everyday life, some without a care in the world; and yet, inside this room, my best friend was fighting for her life.

Marilyn Gives Up the Fight

Late one night, Marilyn started flipping out.

"I can't take it, Carol, I want to die. Look at my body, I am skin and bone. Who will ever want me? I'm ugly." She was trying to get out of the bed. "I am getting out of here! Call someone to pick me up. I can't stand being in here anymore!"

I tried to settle her down, but she was adamant about leaving. I rushed out and told the nurse. Within minutes, the nurse came rushing in with a shot for her. After the injection, Marilyn drifted off into a sedated sleep.

"That ought to keep her for the night," the nurse said, "the doctor has increased her medication."

I pulled my chair close to the bed and gazed at my sick friend. I whispered a desperate prayer, "God, please make Marilyn well. Please let my prayer be the one that gets her up and out of this sick bed. Please!" I leaned over and pressed my lips to her damp forehead. I rubbed her temples. I took her limp hand in mine and held it to my heart.

As the hours passed, I found it impossible to leave her. I wiped her face with a cool rag. When she stirred, I jumped. I sang to her, fluffed her pillow and adjusted the blankets. Finally, I fell asleep clutching her hand.

Marilyn is Dead

It was the second week of September; I was eight months pregnant. Marilyn was sleeping most of the time. She rarely stayed up for more than two hours. Still, I kept a vigil next to her bed.

A nurse came in and found me sleeping in the lounge chair. "Why don't you go on home, honey, you need your rest. Come on, get up and go on home."

I did not want to leave, but I knew I needed to sleep in my own bed. My stomach was huge and my ankles were swollen. I decided I would go home for the night and return first thing in the morning.

"You sure she is all right, Nurse?"

"Yes, dear, we will take good care of her. Now go on home."

On my way out of the room, I paused and glanced back at Marilyn. She looked so still lying there. I walked back in and put my face close to hers.

"I love ya girl, you know that, right?" I kissed her cheek and then walked back out the room. I made my way down on the elevator and out the door.

As I drove away from the hospital, I felt a strange sensation, like a vague terror. It was a fear that Marilyn was letting go of this life.

About seven o'clock in the morning, the phone rang. It was Marilyn's mother.

"Carol, Marilyn died this morning at five a.m." Her voice was somber.

"No, I was with her last night; she was fine."

"She's gone, Carol."

I hung up the phone and stood there, cradling my swollen belly. I let out a sob and hammered the wall with my fists. *I failed you, Marilyn! I could not keep you alive. All my prayers were useless. I failed you, my precious friend, just as God has failed me, again!*

Time to Say Goodbye

At the viewing, I sat staring at my best friend in the casket. After everyone left, I locked the funeral home door so that I could be alone with her. She looked still and peaceful; all the pain she had suffered was now gone.

I reached in the casket and touched her cold, rigid cheek. "Marilyn, it's time to say goodbye. I will never forget you, my dear friend."

In my hand, I held a picture of the two of us, taken before she became ill. I placed it in hers. Then I walked out of the funeral home; my heart was turning to stone.

When they buried her on a fall morning, I stood staring at the hole in the ground. That would be Marilyn's final resting place? The thought of it made me sick. After that, I refused to visit the gravesite. I could not imagine her in the cold, dark ground.

Marilyn Returns From the Other Side

It was mid-afternoon on a cool autumn day. Marilyn had been dead for exactly one month. I was sitting on the couch, surrounded by pictures we had taken through the years— years of fun and laughter, before this evil thing invaded her beautiful body and drained it of life.

Suddenly, I heard the sound of footsteps on the stairway leading up to my apartment door. I quietly moved toward the door and listened. I was not in the mood for company. I did not want to see anyone. I wanted to be alone.

I heard it again; it sounded like someone was coming up the stairs. Gently, I turned the knob and cracked open the door to peek out. To my surprise, there was no one there. I closed it and headed back to the couch.

Again, I heard the same sound. I went back and listened closely. Sure enough, someone was coming up the stairs. This time I pulled the door all the way open to get a full view. Nope, there was no one out there. When I started to close it, I felt a gust of wind flow past me, like someone or something rushed by. I stood frozen in the spot. I cannot explain it, but I just knew it was Marilyn.

"Marilyn?" I questioned aloud.

There was no response, but the room was filled with the scent of her favorite cologne.

Could this be happening?

It has to be Marilyn, I reasoned. *Why do I smell her cologne? Why do I feel her presence? Has she come to visit the apartment as she promised? Has she come to give me some sort of message from the other side?*

Then, as quickly as it had come, the same wind swept past me and out the door, slamming it shut from the force.

I walked back into the living room and sat down. I was perplexed. Was it Marilyn, or in my grief over her death, had I imagined the whole thing? Can someone who has passed over to the other side come back to visit the living?

I was convinced she had.

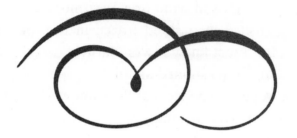

CHAPTER NINE

Adultery and Abortion

A Child is Born

Had she lived, Marilyn would have turned eighteen on October 27th.

My baby was born one day after my best friend's birthday, on October 28th. I didn't know the sex of the baby until it was born. However, the minute I heard the doctor proclaim it was a girl, I whispered, "Her name is Marilynn." When they laid my newborn in my arms, I wept. I had always believed that my best friend would be there for this special day. I longed to share this incredible moment with her.

After the tears of losing her subsided, I wept for joy over my beautiful little baby girl, the new Marilynn! This tiny creature, who had occupied the inside of my abdomen for nine long months, and who took twenty-one long, painstaking hours to come into this world, filled me with wonder.

She was beautiful, with big brown eyes and little rosebud lips. I stroked her and kissed her soft cheeks. Then I made her a promise: "I will be the best Mommy. I will protect you and keep you from harm. And I will always keep you close to me."

A few days later, I left the hospital; I was just eighteen years old.

Lonely

I got a job as a server at a Greek restaurant that was walking-distance from my apartment. My girlfriend Phyllis, who lived next door to me, watched Marilynn while I worked. As soon as I got off, I rushed home to be with my baby. The days were not long enough, but I made every minute count.

Life was blissful and I cherished it, but I was lonely. I decided to give Louie a call. He sounded happy to hear from me, so we made plans to meet that weekend at a local bar.

The minute I sat down, Louie asked about the baby.

"How is she doing? Do you have a picture of her?"

I pulled out a picture and showed it to him.

"I think naming her after Marilyn was really cool, Carol."

As we sat together reminiscing, I could feel the chemistry between us building. He touched my hand, then leaned over and kissed me. I knew what was about to happen and when the time came, I gave myself to him. When the sun came up in the morning, we both went our separate ways. He went back to his life and I returned to mine.

Pregnant Again?

A couple months later, I discovered I was pregnant, again! I didn't know what to do, so I called my mother. When I told her, she did not act surprised.

"Who's the father? Let me guess, Louie?" She was aggravated at my stupidity. "How do you intend to care for two babies? Marilynn is only four months old and you have a job!"

I was not looking for a speech; I just wanted an answer to my dilemma.

She told me about a retired nurse that performed abortions.

"Okay, can I have her number, Mom?"

She rattled it off.

I made the call. When the nurse answered the phone, it sounded like she didn't trust me. And rightly so, this woman was performing illegal abortions on women and charging a couple hundred dollars. She agreed to do it, provided I was alone and told no one about it. We made an appointment for the following Friday. My stomach was in a knot for the rest of the week.

An Old Decrepit Woman

At ten-thirty sharp on Friday morning, there was a knock on the door. I opened the door to see an old decrepit woman standing there—I was aghast.

She spied the apartment suspiciously and asked, "Are you alone, young lady?"

"Yes, I am," I assured her.

"I want my money first."

I went into the bedroom and collected the stack of bills off the dresser. She grabbed it out of my hand and started counting it. When she was satisfied it was all there, she set down her purse and removed her coat.

"Okay, get that baby put away, get into the bedroom and take everything off from your waist down, then lay on the bed."

I gave Marilynn a warm bottle and put her in the crib. When that was done, I stood in front of the old woman, wringing my hands.

"Well don't just stand there; go on and get undressed!"

In the bedroom, I removed my jeans and panties and laid them in a neat pile on the floor. I crawled up on the bed and lay flat on my back. "I'm ready, ma'am."

A Quick Fix

When she entered the room, terror gripped me; her form in the doorway cast a dark shadow over me.

"Scoot down," she ordered, grabbing my ankles and yanking me toward the edge of the bed.

I was shaking like a leaf in the wind.

"Better settle down, girl, can't have you vibrating all over the place; don't want to slip up."

Out of her big dirty purse, she pulled a brown paper bag. I was looking for some clean sterile instruments; however, there were none. She had instead a rubber tube and a long piece of wire. My blood ran cold.

"Will it hurt?" I asked meekly.

"Not too much, haven't had any complaints. Are you planning on being the first?"

I examined her closely as she began her operation. Her face resembled a piece of leather, rough and covered with deep wrinkles. She had dark beady eyes, coarse thinning gray hair and her teeth were dingy and yellow. I wondered if she was going to put on surgical gloves, or at least wash her hands. She didn't. Her hands were knotted at the joints; they looked all crippled up and her fingernails were dirty. I felt sick. I squeezed my eyes shut and tried to think about something else.

The Yellow Rubber Tube

The old nurse was working quickly. I felt her probing, digging and shoving the cold rubber tube up my vagina.

"Oh my God, that hurt," I moaned. The pain shot up my back like fire, and then I felt a pin prick.

"Be still, girl," she said.

I wanted to throw up. My insides were hot; beads of sweat ran down my face.

Then I heard her voice. "Okay, now, get up slowly."

I opened my eyes; she had her hand extended to help me sit up. My lower back felt like it had heavy weights on it. As I started to get up, a rush went to my head; I fell back on the bed. I was sure that I would pass out.

"Don't you go fainting on me, girl," she said harshly.

After a few minutes and a glass of water, I felt somewhat better.

She shoved her utensils into her nasty old purse and grabbed her coat. As she slipped it on, she began shooting orders at me. "Don't lift anything today that could lead to hemorrhaging. Try to sleep as much as possible; your body will need plenty of rest. Also, leave the tube in for twenty-four hours, then take it out and discard it. There will be blood, maybe a lot, maybe not, but don't panic; that's the baby coming out." Her voice had no emotion.

I felt like my heart was going to break in two.

She made her way to the door. "Remember, if anything goes wrong, I don't know you and you don't know me; I was never here, do you understand?"

When she was gone, I stood in the middle of the kitchen, looking around and wondering if I dreamed this completely horrible nightmare.

That night my lower back ached, and the pain from the inserted tube was constant. Twenty-four hours later, just as the old nurse had said, I began to bleed profusely. I removed the rubber tube and tossed it into the garbage.

The next day, I sat in the middle of the living room floor and stared at the wall. *So that's how it goes with abortion,* I thought. *Here one day, gone the next.*

I Am Different

Something happened inside of me that day—I changed. I tried to convince myself that the abortion was the right thing to do, but I could not shake the guilt. I could not put it out of my mind.

To ease my conscience, I started drinking heavily. Because I stayed drunk, I could not make it to work, and so they fired me. Without an income, I could not pay my bills; thus, I was evicted from my apartment two months later.

In desperation, I called my mother and asked her if I could move in with her. Ordinarily, she would have flatly refused, but because of the baby, she agreed.

The World of Drugs

I was spending a lot of time in bars, drinking. In fact, that was all I did. My sister Debbie was taking care of Marilynn at my mother's house.

One night some friends introduced me to the world of drugs. That was the first time that I felt the effects of a drug on my mind and body, and I loved it! The drugs numbed me. When under their influence, I did not feel the guilt of murdering my unborn baby.

One morning, after being gone for five days, without a

word as to where I had been, I stumbled into my mother's house. I flopped down on the bed and passed out. When I crawled out the next afternoon, I went through the house looking for Marilynn.

"Where is my daughter?"

My mother walked over and slapped my face. "*Your* daughter? Or do you mean *Debbie's* daughter, because your sister has been raising that baby for the last three months!"

"Just tell me, where is Marilynn?"

"She's gone."

I went crazy. "Where have you put her?"

"That child is in a safe place with a family that will take care of her."

"How could you do that, Mom? How could you let them take my baby away?"

"I didn't do anything, Carol; you did it to yourself. What kind of mother are you?"

I answered her with resentment dripping off my words, "I am the same kind of mother that you were, useless and absent!"

"Get out of my house!" she screamed. "You're a worthless tramp; now get your rags and get out of here!"

I grabbed a garbage bag, threw my clothes into it and walked out the door, slamming it behind me.

Mikki and I Move In Together

My girlfriend Mikki and I moved into a little cottage apartment. She had just turned eighteen. I worked at a local factory in the office, and Mikki had a very good-paying job in a corporate business office. Between the two of us, we were able to buy some furniture, decorate the cottage and eat well. On weekends, we drank and popped pills. We were living for the moment and partying hard.

I worked with a girl named Kendra. She pretended to like me, but in fact, she saw me as a low-class loser. Personally, I did not care what she thought. I worked to collect a paycheck, not win any points with some office girl.

While sitting at my desk one day, a gorgeous guy came strolling in.

"Kendra, is the boss in?" he inquired.

She nodded, "Yes, Luke."

He passed by me and went into the boss's office.

"Wow, who is that?" I asked.

"Oh, that's Luke Templeton, but don't get too excited; he's married to a friend of mine and has three kids."

I shrugged, "So what? No harm in looking."

Luke

Two days later, I was alone in the office, filing some papers when Luke came in.

"I don't think we have met," he said as he extended his hand to me, "I'm Luke."

"I'm Carol." I could feel my heart pounding as I shook his hand. "Do you work in the building?" I asked him.

"Yes, I maintenance the heating and cooling systems," he answered.

The following week, he showed up again. Kendra was out sick.

"Carol, do you have plans for lunch? I know this fabulous Italian restaurant that serves great shrimp and linguine."

I smiled. "Now, Luke, Kendra said you are *very* married

and I was to stay clear of you."

He laughed. "Kendra needs to mind her own business. Pick you up at twelve-thirty?"

I nodded, "Okay, sounds good." I was shaking when he left. I could barely keep my mind on my work.

At twelve-thirty sharp, he showed up and we did lunch. It began with an innocent lunch, then another, and eventually became long dinners at hideaway places.

Adultery

One night after dinner and drinks, Luke suggested we take a ride to the lake.

He parked the car in a secluded area near the water and turned to me and said, "You're a very attractive girl, Carol. I had my eye on you for a while."

I looked out at the lake; the moon cast a silver shadow on it. The night was spectacular. I got out of the car and walked over to the water's edge. Luke followed behind. We stood there taking in the sights. Sailboats gently made their way to the dock. The scent in the air was intoxicating. Luke reached over, took my hand and squeezed it gently.

"Carol, I want you, do you understand?"

"Of course I do, Luke, but you are a married man."

"My marriage is in name only," he told me.

We walked back to the car and got in. Then he reached for me; suddenly, we were locked in a passionate embrace. Before I knew it, we were climbing into the back seat.

After it was over, I adjusted my clothing and got back into the front seat. Luke drove back to my car in silence. I got out and he drove off.

Mikki's Warning

After that night, I did not see Luke at the office for several weeks.

At home, I hemmed and hawed about how I missed him and wanted to see him again.

Mikki seemed amused. "Hey, no offense Carol, but you can't be serious about a long-term relationship with this guy; he is married, a lot older, and he has kids! Wake up!"

I tried to explain to her that Luke's marriage was in name only.

She laughed, "That's what they all say. Don't be snowed under, Carol; the guy is playing you, plain and simple!"

It was Monday afternoon. The air conditioner had stopped working and the temperature in the office was ninety degrees. We were all sweltering from the heat. To my astonishment, in walked Luke; when I saw him, I about fell off my chair. Kendra caught the look on my face. His wife was her friend, and she resented my attraction to him.

"So Luke, how is your pretty wife?" she questioned.

"My family is doing well," he responded.

I acted unaffected, but being in the same room with him was overwhelming.

When he finished the repair, cool air came rushing through the ducts.

Kendra expressed her elation, "Oh finally, relief! It's been awful hot in here, don't you think, Carol?"

I knew she was being facetious; I didn't reply.

Luke gathered his tools and left.

The next day around lunch, my phone rang; it was Luke.

"I have to see you, Carol, tonight at the same place."

Click, he hung up.

When I got home from work, I looked in my closet for something to wear. I wanted to look great for him. I settled on a sexy-fitting sundress that showed off my tan. I slipped on a pair of strappy sandals and accented the outfit with cute dangling earrings. About this time, Mikki came in.

"Carol, this is going to backfire on you. You're playing with fire!"

"Mikki, that is not true; Luke loves me."

"Carol, you are delirious," she replied.

Used

Luke was sitting at the bar sipping vodka and iced tea when I came in. He stood up when I approached him, left money on the bar for his drink, took my arm and headed for the door.

"Hey, what's the hurry?" I asked.

"I only have a few hours. Let's go to the lake."

When we got to our parking spot, Luke took me quickly; when he was finished, he climbed back behind the wheel and started the car.

"What just happened here, Luke?" I asked, rushing to get dressed.

"I just have to get home, that's all," he said nervously.

As he drove back to my car, I tried to talk to him. "So have you missed me? How are you doing? Where have you been for so long?"

He did not answer any of the questions. He dropped me off at my car and sped off. I stood in the parking lot, watching his car disappear around the corner. I had the distinct feeling that I was being used.

Don't Mistake This for Love, Carol

Then, weeks later, Luke called again.

"Carol, I have to see you. I will pick you up tonight at seven."

When I hung up the phone, Mikki was standing there.

"Please tell me you aren't going to meet him. The guy is using you, Carol, don't you get it?"

I shook her off. "Mind your own business, Mikki, I got this covered."

Luke pulled up to the house right on time. He drove directly to a hotel.

"Aren't we going to have some dinner first?" I asked him.

"I only have a few hours," he told me.

After he finished with me, he got up and dressed quickly.

"Come on, let's get out of here."

"What's wrong, Luke? You have been acting strange toward me."

He sat down in the chair and explained, "Carol, you're only twenty-one years old. I am thirty-eight and I have kids at home. We both walked into this with our eyes wide open. I think we better stop while we are ahead!"

"No, Luke, don't say that. I love you."

"Stop it; don't turn this into a drama. Do not confuse what we had with love. Besides, I never said that I loved you."

Dumped

He drove me home without speaking. When we got to my house, he got out of the car and walked around to my side. He opened the door for me to get out and said, "Relax, Carol, you'll get over me when the next guy comes along."

A feeling of disgust came over me. "*The next guy?* You used me, Luke, and now you are throwing me away."

"The truth is, Carol, we used each other!"

He got back into his car and drove off. I was shattered.

Shortly after Luke broke it off, Kendra put a buzz in his wife's ear about the affair. By now, everyone in the office was talking about it.

His wife showed up at the office, ready to take my head off.

"You little slut, you seduced my husband. We have three children at home—how could you do that? Tramps like you are a dime a dozen!"

I thought she was going to hit me. Had she, I would not have lifted a finger to stop her because I knew I had it coming. However, the woman had too much class to lower herself to my level. When she finished telling me off, she stormed out.

One week later, I heard that Luke resigned from his job. I never heard from him again.

Pregnant, Desperate and Drastic Measures

Two months later, I began losing my breakfast in the toilet.

Yep, I was pregnant and it was Luke's baby. Mikki found me in the bathroom puking.

"Please tell me you are not pregnant."

I looked up from the toilet seat where I was resting my head. "Mikki, what am I going to do?"

She was shocked. "It's that married guy's, isn't it? Carol,

what were you thinking?"

I felt too awful to dwell on how I had ended up in this predicament; I simply wanted to figure out how to get out of it. After she left for work, I sat on the floor, wracking my brain and trying to come up with a solution to "end this inconvenience!"

I spent the next several days attempting to remedy the situation. I heard that hot internal douches worked, so I tried them. I sat in extremely hot baths and took large doses of quinine pills. In desperation, I suggested to Mikki that she kick me in the stomach. She looked at me as if I were insane.

"Have you gone totally crazy, Carol?" she yelled. "You are taking life-threatening risks! Will you please stop trying to abort this baby? You could puncture your uterus and bleed to death." She stood to her feet. "There are ways to deal with this other than trying to use hot internal washes, hangers, or having someone kick you in the stomach!" She went in her bedroom and slammed the door.

The Attempted Miscarriage

I had to get back to my job. I was missing many days. I knew if I kept it up, they would fire me. So, after puking almost every morning, I forced myself to get dressed and go in. At lunch, I called Mikki.

"I have an idea. I think it will work," I said in a whispered tone.

"And what is that, Carol?" she questioned.

"I am going to throw myself down the stairs in the back of the building. I am sure it will cause me to miscarry."

"What if you get hurt or killed?" I could hear the panic in her voice.

"Killed?" I laughed, "At this point in my life that would be a fair escape!"

Mikki tried to reason with me; I hung up the phone.

At eleven-thirty, the crew headed out for lunch. Not to my surprise, I was not invited. I knew the majority of them considered me a home wrecker. After they left, I headed for the back of the building. I opened the heavy door. There was a set of stairs that led down to a glass exit door. It was a long way to the bottom and the steps were steep.

For a moment, I thought I was going to chicken out. However, I was determined to do this. What choice did I have? None! I clutched my belly, closed my eyes and jumped. My body went bouncing down like a ping-pong ball, twisting and turning. When I hit the bottom, I blacked out.

I Didn't Fall, I Jumped

I woke up in the hospital. There was a nurse at my side.

"Well you're awake; let me get the doctor." She pulled up the side rail on the bed and off she went.

I felt a pain in my right leg. I looked down; it was not broken, but it was sore. There was an IV in my arm and a bedpan nearby.

A grey-haired doctor entered the room. He was holding my chart.

"Hello, Ms. Thompson, how are you feeling? You took a serious fall, and it's a miracle that you are okay. Other than the much-bruised leg, you will heal fine. Did you know you were dehydrated?"

I responded flippantly, "No, I did not. Did you know that I am pregnant?"

He looked surprised. "No, I didn't. Are you sure?"

"Of course I am sure. That's the reason that I threw myself down the stairs—to cause a miscarriage!"

The doctor's face turned red. "Are you telling me that you threw yourself down those stairs to abort your baby?"

"You got that right," I answered smugly. "I need an abortion, and if you don't give me one, I'll do something drastic."

The doctor walked over and pointed down at me. "Now you listen to me, young lady. Suicide is against the law and if you try that in this hospital, I will have you committed. Do you understand?"

I sat up in the bed and pointed right back at him. "No, you listen to me, Doctor. If you don't give me the abortion, I will jump off the roof of this hospital, or I'll go home and do it, and this time I won't botch it up!"

Minutes later, the nurse returned with a syringe in her hand. "Roll over and pull up that gown," she ordered me.

"What is that for?" I asked as I lifted my hospital gown to expose my thigh.

"It is valium," she replied.

Well, I thought, *guess the old doctor took me serious.*

Dr. Number One

Early the next morning, a psychiatrist came into the room.

"My name is Dr. Stevens; I am here to talk to you about your attempted suicide." He opened a chart and clicked his pen into action. "Carol Thompson, may I ask you a question? Why do you feel that killing yourself is a way to exterminate a pregnancy?"

I shook my head from side to side and asked myself, *Is*

this guy kidding? I reached over and took a sip of my orange juice and then I answered him. "The truth is I can't have a baby. I have no way to take care of it, and I refuse to carry one full term and then hand it off."

He never flinched. "Actually, I am here to try to help you and possibly get this problem solved."

I grabbed the remote and clicked on the television.

The doctor snatched it out of my hand and clicked it off. "The hospital is considering granting you a therapeutic abortion. Do you know what that is, Carol?" He tapped his trusty pen on the chart, waiting for my answer.

"An abortion is an abortion, termination, death to the fetus," I answered.

He explained, "This hospital feels that if you are a threat to the unborn child, or if the child is a threat to you, we will grant a 'therapeutic abortion.' But before we make that decision, you have to be evaluated by another one of our psychiatrists." He was jotting notes on my chart. "There will be another doctor in to see you tomorrow. Please try to remember that we didn't get you into this predicament, Miss Thompson. It appears you did that yourself."

Dr. Number Two

The next morning, bright and early, as I was finishing my runny eggs and cold toast, there was a gentle tap on the door.

"It's open," I called out.

A doctor walked in, read the name on the chart and inquired, "Carol Thompson?"

"None other," I replied.

"I'm Doctor Nelson; it is nice to meet you, Carol."

This doctor, unlike the one before him, was young, good looking and he had a sweet bedside manner. It made it hard for me to be mean to him. When he finished asking me a bunch of questions, he sat down on the chair next to my bed. His voice was soft and caring.

"Tell me, why are you endangering your life and the life of your unborn child? You could easily carry it to full term and then give it up for adoption; a lot of good people are looking for children to adopt."

"Yeah, Doctor, I am aware of that; the state has already taken my first child from me and she is fostered. I don't want to carry a baby nine months and then turn it over to a stranger—no thanks!"

The handsome young doctor set his chart and pen on the table. Then he scooted his chair up closer to me. He looked directly into my eyes. "Carol, I am here to try to help you. Do you want to talk to me about the things that are troubling you? Or why you tried to take your life?"

His tender voice and gentle manner made me feel defenseless. I thought about letting him in and talking to him. However, I decided not to. Why bother, he could not help me. Besides, I had given up trusting men. Luke took care of that.

I Am Already Dead

"Listen, Doc, if you really want to save what little life I have left in me, then grant me the abortion. Because one way or another, I will terminate this pregnancy, and if it means dying in the process, then so be it!"

The young doctor lowered his head; I sensed sadness in his voice. "Tell me, young lady, what is it that hurts so badly?"

I looked at his handsome face and answered, in barely a whisper, "You wouldn't understand. No one can help me, Doctor, I'm already dead!" I waved my hand at him, signaling him to leave. I turned my face to the wall and refused to say anymore.

Abortion Granted

Later that day, I was informed that the hospital agreed to do a therapeutic abortion.

The night before the procedure, I lay on the bed, motionless. I was empty, void of feeling and cold as ice. I wanted it over—the sooner the better. The thought of Luke and nights of passion with him now seemed ugly to me. His words were lies, he used me for sex and he never cared; no, not for a moment! I was a fool who believed his lies and fell into the trap. I felt a deep searing hatred for him, and it burned a hole in my heart.

Outside the room, I could hear the nurses talking about me. "Give Carol Thompson her shot of valium so she sleeps. She is due in surgery at seven a.m."

I had my gown already pulled back when a nurse arrived with the shot.

"Most people don't like needles," she told me as she stuck me in the hip.

"Not me," I bragged, "don't bother me one bit, feels good actually."

The nurse broke the tip off the hypodermic needle and tossed it in the plastic deposit box. "I suggest you get some help when you get out of here in a few days," she said.

"And I suggest you mind your own business," I shot back.

It Was a Boy

The next morning, I was wheeled into the operating room where I was given a D and C.

When I woke, a nurse was next to the bed puttering around.

"What was it?" I asked, still groggy from the anesthetic.

She ignored my question and continued to tuck in the sheets and fill my water cup.

"Please, can you tell me what it was?" I pleaded.

She put the cup with a straw near my lips, and said "Try to take a sip of this."

I took a tiny drink.

She placed the cup next to my bed. As she was walking out, she paused. "It was a boy; now try to get some rest." She turned out the light and closed the door.

I reached down and stroked my stomach. This morning there was a tiny bump there; now it was gone. Cruel thoughts filled my head. *I am a murderer. First an old woman with a wire and rubber tube, and now this pregnancy, terminated in a clean sterile hospital. What's the difference? It is still two babies.*

The sleeping medication did not work that night. I tossed, turned, and cried bitterly. When the morning came, I hated myself for aborting my baby and I resented God for letting me get pregnant again.

CHAPTER TEN

Heroin, My New Best Friend

Mikki, I Have a Great Idea

When I came home from the hospital, Mikki greeted me with some news:

"They fired you."

I laughed, "So, I am unemployed, oh well, whatever."

Mikki was not amused. "Listen, Carol, you need to get a job. I can't pay the bills on my salary."

I tried to put her at ease. "Hey, Mikki, don't sweat the small stuff. I will get a job, relax!"

I tried to hide it, but emotionally, I was a basket case. For weeks, I had terrible nightmares. I dreamed that a gang of nurses surrounded me; they were chanting, *Murderer! Murderer!*

Mikki woke me up. "Carol, you're having a bad dream."

"I'm okay," I told her, "seems I am having a lot of them lately."

After sitting around the house and getting high for two weeks, I decided we needed a change of scenery, and so I came up with an idea.

"Mikki, why don't we go to New York City for the weekend? It's a holiday and you have Monday off, so let's go have some fun in the Big Apple."

She turned over in her bed. "You're nuts. I have a job, and you should consider looking for one too, Carol."

"Just for the weekend, Mik, it will be a hoot. We can leave next Friday and stay for a few days. It's just seven hours away."

Mikki got up and went into the bathroom.

I followed her in.

"Do you mind? I am trying to pee."

I laughed, "Come on, Mikki, loosen up; we can do this. Don't you want to see the Big Apple?"

Mikki Gives In

I didn't let up, and after hounding and nagging, Mikki caved and gave in.

"Just three days, Carol; I have to be back at my job, and you need to look for one, understood?"

"Yes, of course," I promised.

I persuaded a guy that I knew to give us a ride to the city. I gave him the impression we would all party together once we got there. He was bored and looking for a good time, so he agreed. However, as soon as he drove into the East Village, we jumped out of the car and claimed that we had to go to the john. We cut through to the next street and ditched him.

We found ourselves on a street called St. Mark's Place. It was a wild and drug-infested area, with palm readers, witchcraft paraphernalia shops, restaurants and java shops. We grabbed ourselves a piece of the best pizza I have ever tasted and planted our butts on a set of stairs.

Tall, Dark and Dangerous

As we sat there chomping on our pizza, I spotted a gorgeous guy. He caught me staring at him and came over to us.

His first words were "You're a Sagittarius, aren't you?"

"How did you know that?" I asked, surprised at his accuracy.

"Oh, I just know these things. So tell me, where are you from?"

"What makes you think we are not from here?" I asked.

"Trust me, you're not from here. That is for sure."

I told him we were from Buffalo and we were visiting for the weekend.

"So, what are your plans for the night?" he inquired.

"We haven't any plans, just a few bucks and nowhere to sleep."

"Well, my name is William Brody, but people call me 'Billy.' And what, may I ask, are your names?"

I made the introductions. After we all were acquainted and talked for a while, Billy made a suggestion.

"Hey, listen, I have an idea. Let's go to my friend Jesse's house. He lives right up the street. We can get high and spend the night; sound like a plan?"

Mikki and I agreed. We were tired and needed a place to sleep.

Billy walked us to his friend's house and instructed us to stay outside until he got the "okay." A few minutes later, he was introducing us to Jessie.

"Hey girls," Jesse said, "come on in; heard you are a long way from home and have nowhere to lay your heads." He swept his arm in a gesture for us to go in.

I did not know it then, but it was going to be a night of terror for Mikki.

The Rape

It was a small studio apartment. We sat around and drank cheap wine. Jesse invited Mikki to the back part of the apartment to look at some art. Billy and I stayed in the living room. I dozed off ... but was startled out of my sleep when I heard Mikki's voice; she was crying out for help.

"Stop it, you are hurting me! Carol, make him stop, he is hurting me. Please let me go!"

I jumped up and headed for the back of the apartment.

"I wouldn't do that," Billy said, pulling me back on the floor.

"She needs me, let me go."

Billy grabbed my arm. "She's fine; leave her be. They're just getting acquainted."

I pulled away but he tightened his grip.

"I would advise you to stay here. She is fine, really."

The look in his eyes scared me and the grip he had on me was hurting my arm.

"See, it's quiet now. Your friend is all right. Now, you settle down here with me," Billy said, coaxing me to lie down beside him; so I did.

The next thing I knew, I heard the voice of another girl screaming and yelling.

"What are you doing in my home? Who are you? Where is Jesse?"

I looked up to see a young woman, about twenty-two, standing over us. She turned and ran into the bedroom in the back. I heard her screech, "How could you? And how could you bring these girls in our home?"

Mikki came running out, her clothes disheveled and her

eyes red from crying.

"Get your things," Billy ordered us, "she's having a hissy fit. Let's blow out of here."

When we got a few doors away, I could still hear the girl screaming at Jesse. Billy was snickering and mocking her.

We landed up in a Java House. Billy got us both a coffee and a bagel. Mikki was crying; she shoved the bagel across the table.

"I don't want to eat! I want to go home, now!" She got up and headed for the john; I was right behind her. When we got inside, she let me have it. "You call yourself my friend, Carol," she sobbed, "how come you didn't help me?"

"I wanted to, but Billy wouldn't let me. He said that you were fine."

She turned to me with her eyes blazing. "Is crying and begging someone to stop 'fine'?" She wiped her tears with some toilet tissue. "He raped me repeatedly, and he hurt me." She pulled down her jeans and exposed bruises on her inner thigh.

I was shocked. "Okay, Mikki, we will head home this afternoon."

Don't Ever Call Me Crazy

We started walking through Soho, a trendy village in Manhattan. I told Billy what happened to Mikki. He didn't bat an eye. In fact, he acted as if we were making too much of it.

"Listen girls, this isn't Buffalo, steel plants and polka halls. This is New York City and sometimes things happen."

I was floored; Billy was so obtuse about Jesse raping Mikki and so I confronted him about it.

"How can you be so unaffected? Your friend Jesse raped my girlfriend and you act as if it is nothing. Are you crazy?"

When I said that, something came over him that scared the living daylights out of me! He grabbed my head and pressed his face against mine. His eyes had a wild look.

"Don't you ever call me crazy, you got that?"

"I am sorry, Billy, I didn't mean it," I said apologetically.

His expression softened. "Okay, so what do you say? Should I show you around the city that never sleeps?"

As we walked along, I told Mikki, "We better stick around with him for a while; we are lost in this city, and besides, we have no way home. Give me a day and I will figure out a way to get us out of here, safely."

"Okay," she agreed, "but you better make it fast. I think this guy is insane. Did you see how he acted when you called him crazy?"

Meet Moses

Billy took us out on the ferry to see the Statue of Liberty. As the boat made its way to the site, he informed us of the rich history of the famous statue.

"The Statue of Liberty was a gift to us from France," he explained. "The face of Lady Liberty is the image of the sculptor's mother. The statue was sent here in pieces and then assembled. It took a long time before it was finished. The torch that she holds high in her hand lit the way for the weary immigrants that arrived here after crossing the vast and perilous Atlantic Ocean."

Mikki and I were intrigued.

After our tour, we landed up back in Soho. Then Billy took us to an art gallery. He told us that the place was owned by a drug dealer. After he purchased a bag of pills from the guy, he gave Mikki and I two apiece.

"What are these?" Mikki asked.

"It's speed and it will wind your clock," Billy answered.

As we walked through the rooms, admiring the art and sculptures, the pills took effect. The stuff was strong. Both Mikki and I were speeding our brains out. I went through four packs of chewing gum and chattered non-stop. Mikki stared at the same painting for over an hour.

On my way out of a bathroom, I heard someone groaning. I peeked around the corner into a storage room and spotted a person lying on the floor; he was rolled up in a ball.

"Are you all right?" I inquired.

Billy came up behind me. "Hey Moses, you sick?"

Moses was withdrawing from heroin and it was brutal. Billy completely ignored the agony he was in. I was certain he had seen him like that before.

"Moses, I want you to meet a couple of girls from Buffalo. Found them slumming on St. Marks Place."

Moses looked up at us; he could barely speak.

"Come on, Moses, I'm going to get some dope. I will get you something to take you off empty. Just remember, you owe me!"

Moses got up off the floor. His eyes were blood red; his hair, tousled. His hands were dirty and he was dressed in shabby, wrinkled clothes. He wiped his runny nose (a sign of hard withdrawals) and walked out with us into the cool April air. He needed a shot; he was riding on empty and every muscle and bone in his body hurt.

Check This Place Out

Billy had a blank check that he stole from his father. He forged it and went to a place he knew would cash it. When he came out, he was waving a bunch of hundred-dollar bills. He hailed a cab; we all piled in and we were off. The cab needled through traffic. Billy had the driver drop us off at a place on Second Avenue.

He told us he knew the guy that owned B&W Recording Studios and that he sold high-quality cocaine and heroin. We went up the elevator to the third floor. When the doors opened, I was amazed. It was a beautiful apartment, with high ceilings and rich wood paneling. The floors were covered in oriental rugs and the windows were draped in thick rich fabric. The furniture was gorgeous; wood carved and covered in big colorful toss pillows. There were Waterford Crystal bowls on the tables, each filled with pot. On an ornate table in the center of the room was a beveled glass mirror; on it, lines of coke and a hundred-dollar bill rolled up like a straw, for anyone who wanted a "toot."

We were invited to sit down, relax, and if we wanted, we could help ourselves to all the goodies. Mikki and I had never snorted coke. We had just smoked pot and popped pills. We were about to embark on a new discovery: cocaine and heroin.

After Billy completed the drug transaction, the owner of this prestigious establishment invited us on a tour of his beautiful studio. We got on an elevator and went up to the fifth floor. This time when the doors opened, it was a fully equipped state-of-the-art recording studio. The floors were solid wood and shined like glass. A group was recording their album. We were instructed to be very quiet.

Billy Propositions Me

When the group finished their set, they decided to take a break. Mikki and I were yakking away about how cool the place was. Billy was talking to the owner, who called himself "Phoenix." He called me over and draped his arm around my shoulder.

"Carol, I have a proposition for you, rather flattering if you ask me. Phoenix wants you to stay here for a few days as his guest. He has plenty of money, as you can see. He said he will buy you some nice clothes, and you can do all the drugs you want. What do you say, you game?"

I looked at Phoenix and smiled shyly. "Can Mikki stay too? And will you be here, Billy?"

Billy pulled his arm off me. He had that crazed look in his eyes again. He excused us and dragged me over to the side. "Are you nuts? Do you know who this is? What kind of nonsense is that, 'Can Mikki stay?' Grow up! This is a good deal; he wants some fun and you will make out good. We will be back in a few days, deal?"

I shook my head. "No, Billy, I don't want to be left here alone; I want Mikki with me."

He looked at me as if he wanted to hit me. "This guy is going to give me some extra dope if you remain. Now, I suggest you rethink this."

I started walking away. "I will not be left. I don't even know this guy."

Billy followed behind me. "Listen, here's a news flash for you, Carol: You don't know me either!"

Still, I refused to stay without Mikki. Billy informed Phoenix of my decision and then we left. On the way out, down the elevator and out to the streets, Billy continuously hammered me.

"You could have had it all, you stupid Polish, Buffalo moron!"

Heroin

When night fell, we climbed up onto a secluded staircase and sat down. It was a chilly April night. Below us was a nightclub. We could hear jazz music; it sounded nice. Moses opened a packet of heroin and put it into a spoon. He poured some water out of a bottle into the spoon and dissolved the powder. Then he lit a match and cooked it up. The liquid began to sizzle and boil. He threw a piece of cotton in, and then pulled a hypodermic needle out of a bag. With it, he drew some of the liquid out of the spoon and into the syringe.

He pointed to me. "You first, Carol," he said, "I can't wait to see you on this stuff."

I extended my arm. Needles did not scare me. I think it surprised Moses.

"Your first time?" he asked.

"Yep, my first time," I answered.

Billy tied off my arm with the belt and pulled it snug. Moses examined it for a vein.

"Ah, here's a plump one."

I watched as he plunged the needle in. When he emptied the contents into my arm, a rush ran straight to my head. I felt like I was wrapped in a liquid blanket. It was amazing! I had never felt anything like this with anything I had ever done before. I was floating on a river; my whole body was responding to the opiate-high.

After that first shot, I could not wait for the next.

Billy's Second Proposition

Either we were sitting in an alley nodding out on the heroin, or walking through the streets looking for a place to sleep. The fact is we were out of money, Moses needed a shot and Billy wanted some coke.

Billy asked me if I would do a "skin flick."

"What's a skin flick?" I asked.

"You are one dumb chick," he said, laughing at me. "It's a porn film. They will give us $125.00 apiece!"

I was mortified. "I won't do that, Billy," I protested, "never, not that!"

By the time we got to the apartment in South Bronx, he was seething. I thought he was going to hit me. I covered my face. He backed off but cautioned me, "Not now, but I assure you, Carol, it is coming!"

Things were heating up. The money was gone, Billy was edgy and I was ready to go home.

I told Mikki, "We've been here over a week; let's go, it is getting dangerous. Moses is a thief. Sooner or later he is going to get caught, and Billy scares me."

Mikki was not in a hurry to get home or back to her job anymore. She loved the heroin, and she and Moses were getting cozy.

"This stuff is outstanding, Carol; don't you just love it?" she asked me after we had just shot up.

"Yes, Mikki, I do, but these guys are going to dump us sooner or later. We are not contributing to their drug habits or ours. Billy comes up with all these wild ideas about me doing porn or staying with one of his rich friends for a dope tradeoff!"

Mikki certainly had a different attitude. "Hey, relax, and just say no. Billy will not force you. Besides, I like it here. I will call my job and get a few sick days. Let's hang out for a while longer, okay?"

I was beginning to worry and wonder if my "big idea" to come to the city was not a major mistake.

Lost in New York

We had been walking all day; my feet hurt and I was ready to head home.

"Okay guys, Mikki and I are going home now." I just blurted it out.

"Why do you want to leave and go back to Buffalo?" Billy asked.

"It beats what we're doing here, and furthermore, we left jobs behind. If we get back, we may still have them. Mikki, let's go." I reached out to grab her hand; she stepped back away from me.

"I don't want to leave yet, Carol."

Billy piped in, "You heard her, she wants to stay with Moses. If you want to leave, go!"

"Mikki, you have family; your mother has to be freaking out. Come on, let's go."

She moved closer to Moses; he put his arm around her.

Oh no, this is serious, I thought. "Well, I am going home. Mikki, are you coming?"

She shook her head in response. I tried to reason with her, but she ignored me.

Billy kept nudging me. "Go ahead, go home, Pollock."

I figured that if I started walking, Mikki would follow me. I was wrong. I looked behind me; she was not there. In fact, I could not spot her anywhere in the fast moving crowd. Now I was panicking. New York City is not a place to walk away from someone. In seconds, you can lose sight of them. That is exactly what happened. I was about to find out just how lost I was.

An Officer to the Rescue

Somehow, I found my way back to Broadway. I knew that Moses would eventually show up at the billiards room, selling his stolen property and buying his nighttime stash. He would need it to get him through to the morning. This guy had a major habit! I am talking strung out to the max!

When I occupied a corner to sit around and wait, I was booted off by a prostitute.

"Get the hell out of here before I bust your skull," she threatened me.

I have always been tough and pretty much can hold my own, but these broads were serious, and things being as they were, I did not need the grief, so I obliged her and moved on.

I stood in front of a coffee shop for hours, shivering; still no sign of Mikki. It was about one in the morning. I was shifting into panic mode.

A man approached me.

"I'm a police officer; are you all right?"

"No, I am not; I lost my friend and I don't have a place to stay. I am hungry and cold."

"Come with me," he ordered, pointing to a police car at the curb.

I climbed in the back seat. I was not sure where he was taking me, but I trusted him. He being a police officer and all, I was sure I was safe. He drove up the street to a deli, and then he went inside and bought me a sandwich and coffee. I wolfed the whole thing down.

"Where are you taking me, Officer? Are you going to lock me up?"

"No, on the contrary, I am going to help you."

We pulled up to a hotel. He told me to get out and follow him.

"Don't be afraid; I won't hurt you," he assured me.

We walked down a long hallway; he stopped at a door and knocked three times. It sounded like a signal knock. A young redhead opened the door. When she saw him, she smiled.

"Hey Sam, aren't you on duty? Who's the girl?"

We entered the room. It had an adjoining room and the door was open. I counted four girls and one small baby, about a year old. Sam was very sweet to them, giving them hugs and showing affection.

A Safe Place?

"You will be safe here," Sam told me as he headed for the door. "Just clean up and get some sleep. I will be back in a few hours." He motioned to one of the girls. "This is Jackie; she will take care of you, Carol."

He turned to Jackie. "Make sure that Carol is made comfortable and gets some sleep." They threw each other a knowing look.

The shower felt miraculous. I had not taken one in days. When I came out of the bathroom, the girls were eating pizza and drinking cokes. They offered me a piece, but I was still full from the sandwich.

"What do you girls do for Sam?" I asked.

What a Set Up

They all looked at each other, then Jackie spoke up.

"The four of us have no place to live, so we stay here with Sam. He is a police officer, so it's cool."

I knew there was more, so I pressed on. "Yeah, but how do you support yourselves?"

This time the girl with the baby spoke up. "My name is Tiffany; I have been here for six months. Sam knows some rich men in this city who pay big bucks for a good time. We do that for Sam, show his friends a good time. And in return, Sam gives us a place to live, food to eat and protection from the streets."

I looked all of them over; these girls were young. The four of them were "over-the-top pretty." Tiffany was tiny and petite; she had skin like porcelain. Cathy was dark skinned and beautiful; her body was perfect. Isabella was a beauty as well, long-legged and tall. Her hair was dark and hung down her back. She was very quiet and suspicious of me. Jackie was a knockout, with red hair and green eyes.

Jackie escorted me into the adjoining room and told me I could sleep there. She extended her hand and said, "Here, take these, they're sleeping pills. They'll help you to relax."

I was glad to see those pills. I took them and crawled between the sheets. The bed smelled so good; I snuggled under the warm blanket and thought about my friend Mikki. I hoped she was not doing too much dope. I planned to get up early, get back to Soho and find her!

Sam's Plan to Prostitute Me

As I lay sleeping, I was startled from someone groping me. I turned around; it was Sam. He was lying next to me in the bed.

135

"Stop it," I protested, "Knock it off!"

He got up and went into the next room. I fell back asleep.

I woke up about seven-thirty in the morning. I could hear them talking in the other room. They were unaware that I was awake.

Tiffany was speaking, "Sam, how can you be sure that she will do what we do for you?"

Sam answered her with confidence, "Did you see her arms? Someone has taken a needle to them. She has no place to go. You bet she will be an escort. She'll do exactly what I say or I'll have her locked up."

I got out of the bed and slipped into my clothes. Quietly, I crept over to the door, opened it and took off. I ran down the hallway and out to the street. I had to get back to the village and find Mikki. I was going to get her and insist we go back to Buffalo, even if I had to drag her!

In Search of Mikki

I managed to get a ride to Soho. I did not find Mikki, but I ran right into Billy. He was standing on a street corner, talking to some shady-looking character. I ran over and wrapped my arms around his neck.

He pulled away and said, "Well, Princess, finally back. Where have you been hanging out?"

I told him about my experience with Sam and the girls.

He laughed, "Walked away from making some good money again, did ya? That cop could have set you up. But, as usual, you're too stupid to see a good thing."

I was not interested in his opinions. I just wanted to find Mikki. So I asked him, "Have you seen Mikki?"

"You bet, she and Moses are holed up in an apartment in the Bronx and your little friend is getting hooked."

"Will you take me to her, Billy?" I asked, stroking his neck.

Surprisingly enough, he agreed.

When we arrived, I found Mikki lying in a bed. She had not showered in days. Her hair was greasy and she had black circles under her eyes. She was wasted!

"Hey Carol, you got to get some of this stuff in your arm; it is the best yet," she slurred.

"How much are you giving her, Moses?" I asked.

"Just enough; she's fine, don't worry. Catch her in the morning."

Billy yanked my arm and said, "Come on, let's go. I got some primo stuff. Let's get high."

The Beating

We went into a bedroom down the hall. As soon as we got high, Billy started talking nonstop. He had done some speed earlier and the mixture of the two drugs had him flying and nodding at the same time. His mood was erratic.

"Now that you're back and you realize you need me, Carol, I have come up with a new plan to make some money; it's called the Murphy game. And since you refuse to do porn, I think you will be happy with this idea." He proceeded to explain how the game worked. He would place me on a corner, and then he would strike a deal with a man who would pay for sex with me.

I protested immediately, "I won't prostitute, Billy!"

He reached over and slapped me across the face; I tasted blood. "Shut up," he screamed, "just shut up and do as I say!"

"Leave me alone, Billy," I yelled back at him, "you're a nut job, just a crazy nut job!"

The look on his face was sheer madness. He came at me swinging. *"Crazy?* Is that what you called me? I am going to show you how *crazy* I am!"

He grabbed me by my throat; both his hands tightened around my neck. He dragged me to the window and threatened to throw me out. We were on the thirteenth floor. I could see the cars below speeding by. He had my head pushed out the window; it was raining. When he pulled me in, my face was soaked with rainwater and blood. He still had his hands around my throat in a death grip. My air supply was cut off and I could not breathe. Things were growing dark; I knew I was passing out.

The Beating Continues

Then he released me. He looked like a wild animal in a rage. I ran for the door.

"Mikki, Mikki," I screamed, "help me!"

Billy yanked me back into the bedroom. He balled up his fist and hit me, connecting with my jaw. I felt my tooth crack; blood ran down my busted lip. He hit me again— *crack*! I started spitting out teeth.

He jumped on the bed and continued screaming. "I rule, do you understand, girl? I rule, or I will kill you, sure as you are standing there!"

He then jumped off the bed, pouncing on me. His weight slammed me to the floor.

I tried to crawl away; he grabbed my nightgown and it ripped in his hands. I was still trying to get away. I was naked and badly beaten, but his rage was undiminished. I was screaming and begging him to stop; my blood was splattered everywhere.

"Billy, please stop! You are going to kill me!"

I looked toward the door hoping Mikki and Moses would come and help me, but there was no sign of them.

"Are you calling for your friend?" he asked.

He picked me up by my hair and swung me around. My feet came up off the ground. I landed a few feet away. When I looked up, he was coming at me. His face was that of a madman. I was bleeding badly from my mouth; he had a handful of my hair hanging from his fingers. I was terrified that he was not done!

He grabbed me and when he hit me this time, I flew over a chair and crashed to the floor against the wall. I was sure he had broken a bone in my foot. I rolled up in a ball; the pain was excruciating.

I began to crawl away and begged, "Please, Billy, don't hit me again; I am sorry. I will play your Murphy game, but please don't hit me again!"

This Guy is Going to Kill Me!

He stood over me like a maniac. "You got it now, girl, that's what I want to hear. Now get in the bed." I reached for my nightgown; he pulled the ripped garment away from me. "You're entirely too inhibited, Carol; you have to learn to loosen up. I will teach you how!" He pressed his face against mine, his wild eyes glaring at me. "Get used to it, Carol. You're not in Buffalo now!"

That night Billy raped me. When I cried, he beat me again.

When I woke up the next day, Billy was still sleeping. I could barely move. I crawled out of bed, making sure not to wake him. I tiptoed to the bathroom. When I walked in, Mikki was getting ready to take a shower. She saw my face and gasped. My lip was split wide open, my neck was purple and my left eye was swollen shut. My nightgown was ripped and hanging off one side of my body.

"Didn't you hear me screaming last night?" I asked through bloody lips. "Why didn't you come and help me?"

Mikki looked down at the floor. "Moses told me to mind my own business, and that if I interfered, Billy would beat you worse."

I grabbed her shoulders. "Look at me, Mikki, you should have come. He's a mad man and he could have killed me!"

Mikki pulled away and glared at me. "Don't try to put me on a guilt trip, Carol. Where were you when Jesse raped me? If I remember correctly, Billy told you not to interfere, and you didn't, so don't try to make me feel bad!"

I looked into the mirror. "Oh my God, I look like I have been hit by a bus!" I sat down on the toilet seat. "I want to go home; let's just leave, Mikki, please."

She stripped off her clothes and stepped into the shower. "I don't want to leave Moses. I really care for him."

I pulled back the shower curtain. "You have known this guy a little over a week, are you kidding? Mikki, look at me. Look what Billy has done to me."

She tugged at the shower curtain to close it. "I have to think about it."

The Murphy Game

The next day, to avoid another violent encounter with

Billy, I agreed to play his "Murphy game." He took me to the corner of a street. Then he explained to me what I was to do and how to do it.

"When you see me take the money, I will point to you; that means go into the hotel, but don't go to the room, go out the back door like I showed you and run to the next street. I will meet you there. I'll tell the guy that you are waiting in one of the rooms. Just do as I say; we can make some money and you don't have to prostitute, so relax."

For a few nights, we played the game. However, most of the men were hip to it and refused to pay Billy in advance. They wanted to get to the room and see me there before they put up the cash.

About six in the morning, after being up all night, Billy came rushing into the bedroom.

"Get dressed, we're leaving. I have to go to my parents' house in Yonkers to get some blank checks. We are out of money."

I dared to ask, "Can I stay here with Mikki?"

He grabbed my arm and dug his nails into my flesh. "No, you can't. We are going to get some money. You will see her tomorrow; let's go!"

On our way out of the apartment, I went into the room where I found Mikki lying on the bed. She was wasted. Her eyes were rolled back in her head, in a deep heroin high. Moses was giving her a lot of dope—too much. I am positive he was making sure she was hooked so he could put her out on the streets to prostitute for him.

I went up to her and whispered in her ear, "Mikki, when I get back, we will escape out of this hell that I have brought you to."

The Trip to Yonkers

Billy and I made our way to Yonkers. First, we got on the subway. In between trains, Billy took off to the public john to shoot up. For a fleeting moment, I hoped he would overdose. Then I thought about being alone and lost, so I shook the thought out of my head.

After the subway ride, we started walking again. The air was cold and the wind was blowing; I was freezing. All I had on was a tee shirt and ripped jeans.

Billy decided he needed another shot. It was three in the morning. He had no water to dilute the drugs, so he drew some out of a dirty puddle. I remembered how sick I had gotten with Hep A when I drank the toilet water. I said nothing. I was afraid he would beat me.

After walking for what seemed like miles, Billy talked a bus driver into letting us grab a free ride up to Yonkers. When we got to the neighborhood where he lived with his parents, I was stunned. It was beautiful. The apartment homes were luxurious, and there were tall trees with lush landscapes. In an effort to be nice, I told Billy how lovely the place was.

He looked at me with that wild-eyed expression. "Did you think I came from the slums?"

I was terrified. "No, of course not! I just think this area of New York City is nice."

He grabbed my chin and pressed his fingers into it, holding it tightly. "First of all, this is not New York City, it's Yonkers."

"Of course it is," I said, trying to pull my face out of his grip, "I just thought—"

"You just thought wrong, you stupid girl. Has anyone ever

told you how stupid you are, Carol?" he asked sarcastically.

"As a matter of fact, yes; my mother told me that for years," I answered.

"Well, she was right; you are a stupid person."

I thought to myself, *Yeah and you are one nutcase.* However, I never would have dared to say it aloud. I was still black and blue from the last beating.

Farewell, You Crazy One

"Well, I don't know about you, but I am going home to get some food and sleep," Billy informed me.

I protested, "Billy, you said you were getting checks and then we were going back to Mikki and Moses."

"Well, I guess I lied," he said, snickering like some sort of a devil.

He pulled me close and pressed his lips on mine. I kept my lips pursed.

"Hey, you don't like me anymore?" he joked.

"Please don't leave me here, Billy. I am begging you."

"Well, don't bother begging anymore because I am going home."

With that, he walked up the stairs, put in a code and the door opened.

I slid in the hallway with him, still begging him not to abandon me.

"Goodbye Carol, you've been a real drag. See ya around!" He walked away and disappeared into one of the apartments.

Another Proposition

I was left alone, but this time I was not scared; I was too

cold and hungry to be scared. I went down to the bottom floor of the building and hid there. I must have fallen asleep. The next thing I knew, there was a man staring down at me.

"What you are doing here?" he asked.

I rubbed my eyes to wake myself up.

"You can get into a lot of trouble for loitering on this property, you know."

I was at my wits end. "Please don't call the police. I will leave."

He stopped me. "No, that's okay; come with me."

I followed him to an apartment that was vacant.

"Be very quiet," he told me. "I will be back shortly."

I sat on the floor. The place was huge with floor-to-ceiling windows and chandeliers. Outside, the wind was blowing; the trees swayed in the breeze as if doing some exotic dance. It was morning and the sun was up.

The guy returned about thirty minutes later. He handed me an egg sandwich and warm coffee. I ate it like a starved animal. He sat against the wall and watched me.

He started asking me questions. "So, you are not from here?"

I told him about Buffalo and my lost friend.

"You will not find her so easily in the city," he told me. "That place can gobble a person up, fast!" He came over and sat next to me.

Dear God, don't let this guy be another weirdo, I thought.

"I can take you to a man that will pay you good money for favors," he said. "Would you be interested?"

I began to cry. "No, I just want to go back to Buffalo, that's all I want." I told him about Billy and asked him if he knew him.

"Yes, of course, his parents live in this building. They are very wealthy."

I asked him to do me a favor and go find him for me.

"I can't do that, I would lose my job, but if you are nice to me, maybe I will find a way to get a message to him." He began stroking my leg and making suggestive remarks.

I was terrified.

Busted

Suddenly, the door flew open and three men walked in. The guy jumped up.

"What are you doing in here with this girl?" one of them asked.

"She was wandering around the building; I brought her here and I intended to come and report to you, sir," he answered, his voice shaking.

"You're a liar and you're fired; now get out!"

As the guy scrambled to leave, the man in charge turned to me.

"And you, young lady, what are you doing soliciting yourself on my property?"

I didn't have a hint what "soliciting" meant. I stood there speechless.

For the next fifteen minutes, he threatened me. "You're trespassing and you're a vagrant. You are giving my prestigious property a bad name. You were selling yourself to my maintenance man and I am having you arrested."

I was shaking in my shoes. "Sir—"

Before I could say another word, he cut me off. "Call the police and get this prostitute out of here."

I began to cry. I could not take it anymore; the last

eleven days were hell, total hell! All I could think about was how would I find Mikki and take her home if I was going to jail.

One of the men stepped forward. He was handsome and impeccably dressed. He reached over and placed his hand on the irate owner's shoulder.

"Hold on Charlie, let me have a word with this young girl before you make any drastic decisions, please!" he insisted.

A Gentle Man

The man walked toward me; his eyes were kind.

"What is your name and how old are you?" he asked.

"My name is Carol Thompson and I am twenty-one years old."

"Is that the truth?"

"Yes, it is!"

"Do you have any identification?"

"No," I replied, "I am from Buffalo."

"I am not trying to scare you, Carol, but you know you are in trouble. Your arms are bruised from needles; it is obvious you are a drug user and you have no I.D. You are loitering on private property and you are being accused of soliciting sex. These are serious violations, young lady." He examined my badly beaten face and neck. "Tell me, who beat you up? It looks like you have been choked."

I was silent.

He asked one of the men standing there to go and find out the price of a train ticket from New York City to Buffalo.

Today, I Am Going to Save Your Life

He then turned to me and said, "Today, I am going to save your life because if you stay in the city, you will probably die. I am going to plant a seed in your life, a one-way ticket back to Buffalo." He put his hand under my chin and lifted it up to look into my eyes. "You see, Carol, I have a sixteen-year-old daughter and if she ever gets into a situation like this, I pray someone will do for her what I am about to do for you!"

The man returned. "There is a train going to Buffalo at three-fifteen this afternoon; the cost is fifty-three dollars."

The kind man reached into his pocket and took out the fifty-three dollars. "Take her to the station and make sure she gets on that train."

Then he turned and faced me. "Go home, young lady."

On the way to the train station, I questioned the driver, "Who was that man who paid for my ticket?"

"Oh, that is Mr. Brandon. He is a wealthy businessman. He is always doing things like this; he is a Christian."

The Long and Winding Road

I boarded the train and took a seat next to the window. The train pulled out of the station and started to pick up speed. I watched as the scenery raced past me. I was safe, but my heart was aching. I had left Mikki behind. I was the one who talked her into leaving her job and going to New York City. It was my fault that she was raped; I was supposed to take care of her. I was the one who took the first shot of heroin; she saw how I liked it so she did it too. Instead of protecting her, I abandoned her in New York.

I was getting a clear picture of myself: evil and cunning,

147

selfish and conniving. I had failed Mikki, just as I had failed Marilyn, my daughter, and my two unborn babies.

I laid my head back on the seat and let out a moan.

The woman seated next to me asked, "Are you all right, honey?"

"No," I answered, "I am a bad person; I have left my friend in the city to die."

She turned and looked the other way.

Trashed

I arrived home late that night. The front door of the cottage was wide open. The place was a mess! My bedroom was full of garbage and litter. The kitchen had dirty dishes everywhere, the linoleum was ripped up, and the furniture was gone. Someone had carried out the couch and chair. Our clothes were missing and there were obscenities written on the walls.

I sat on the floor and looked around at the trashed house. I figured there was only one thing for me to do: go out and get high. However, pills would not be enough—not anymore. I had tasted the opiate, heroin. That was what I needed. I went out to the streets to find it and discovered it was easy to obtain. In fact, there was a dealer right up the street who was more than willing to fill my "order."

CHAPTER ELEVEN

The Psych Ward

I Am Crazy

I had been home from New York City for a couple of weeks, most of which I do not remember because I was out of it the whole time. I was shooting up regularly and hanging with the worst drug addicts in the city.

I returned to the house where Mikki and I had lived. There was an eviction notice tacked to the door and a padlock. I was homeless. My old friend Betty usually let me stay at her house; we had been friends in high school. However, that welcome ran out when she realized that I was addicted to heroin.

Every day I lived in constant torment about Mikki. I detested myself for having left her in New York. It got to the point where I could not look at my reflection in the mirror. I asked myself the same questions every day. *Has she overdosed? Is she prostituting to keep up with her habit? Is she waiting for me to come back and get her? Is she dead?*

The more I thought about it, the more dope I shot. I felt like I was going crazy; the truth is I was!

One afternoon while wandering the streets, I was picked up and committed to the Psych Ward in a mental hospital. I had suffered from a total nervous breakdown.

When I woke up in the "cell," a nurse greeted me.

"Where am I and how did I get here?" I asked.

"You, my dear, are a very sick girl." She gave me a shot; it knocked me out cold.

Hepatitis B

Three doctors came in to see me the next day. They informed me that I had Hepatitis B.

"We are aware you are an IV user and I suspect your liver is damaged. However, we would have to do a biopsy to be certain. You are dehydrated, undernourished and suffering from a mental breakdown."

The next doctor picked up where he left off. "Are you addicted to heroin, Carol?"

"No, of course not," I replied.

He knew I was lying. "Well, you will be going through some withdrawals; we will try to help as much as we can. You will be here for a while, so relax and try to get well."

They looked at each other to see if anyone had anything else to add.

"No? Okay then, we are finished here."

With that, they turned and walked out. The door of the "cell" was locked.

Within hours, I was freaking. I refused food; I was shaking and begging for some medicine. I was given one pill a day and it did nothing!

I was not allowed visitors. Again, I was left alone, just like when I had the Hep A. I fell into major depression and confusion. Without drugs to numb me, I was sure this place would be my coffin.

My Meltdown

After two weeks of hell in isolation, my withdrawals were subsiding and I was finally allowed visitors. Will Means, an old friend from school, came to see me regularly. When he asked about Mikki, I freaked out, so he quickly changed the subject. Sometimes when he came to see me, he would find me standing on the bed acting like a cat. Other times, I yelled obscene comments and made lewd gestures. As I remember, Will was the only one who visited me during my stay in the "nut house." At times like that, you can count your real friends on one finger.

Sleeping had become almost impossible. I cried all night and ranted all day. Finally, I was put on close watch. I lay on my bed day after day, wishing I were dead. I hated myself and everything I stood for, which was nothing! My days were filled with loneliness. I had nightmares all the time. I would wake up in the middle of the night, drenched in sweat. I dreamed of the babies I aborted; they were reaching for me, crying. Other dreams were of Marilyn, my best friend; she too was reaching for me, begging me to help her. I would see visions of Mikki lying in a gutter, her eyes staring up at me, lifeless. Sometimes I would have nightmares of my daughter, Marilynn; in them, she would be screaming at me for not being there for her.

My Little Companion

Early one morning, I crawled out of bed and walked over to the window. I looked out; it was a strange view. My room faced an octagon brick wall. Only when I looked up did I see the sky. Below was an overgrown courtyard. There were tables and chairs, flower pots and fancy trimmed ledges where plants once grew.

A small yellow bird was flying around in the courtyard. He landed on my windowsill. I went over to my bed and lay down so I could watch him. He flew away, leaving behind one single yellow feather. I picked it up and ran it down along my cheek. I put it under my nose to catch a scent of the little bird. I kept the feather on my bedside table.

To my delight and surprise, he returned the next morning. I sat and watched him hop around on the windowsill. I was careful not to make any quick movements, as I was afraid I would scare him off.

That night, I left bread crumbs for him, in case he came back, and he did. The little guy seemed delighted when he discovered the little treats. He watched me as he ate. Afterwards, his golden throat swelled up and he let out a lovely song. Then he fluffed his sunshine-colored wings and flew away.

The company of my little companion was the only thing I had to look forward to. He was the highlight of my lonely days. One morning, he came early. The sound of his song woke me. I made little sounds in my throat trying to imitate him. He made them back. For a fleeting moment, the thought crossed my mind that maybe "God" sent this little friend to remind me that I was not forgotten.

In the Courtyard Below

The next day, he did not show up. The day after, there was still no sign of him. I was beginning to wonder where he was. I sat at the window, looking up at the sky above and the enclosed courtyard down below. That is when I saw him. He must have hit the wall and fell to his death. I was stricken with grief. I crawled into my bed and lay there for days, unable to eat or drink. My precious little friend, who had visited me faithfully and cheered me up with his lovely songs, was dead. I thought God had sent him; instead, I was sure that it was God who had taken him away.

Going Home, Where's Home?

"You're going home today, Miss Carol!" It was the nurse.

"I am? You mean I'm not nuts anymore?"

She chuckled, "Guess not, your release is being signed as we speak."

When she left the room, I sat on the chair and asked myself, "Where is home?"

I walked out of the hospital at twelve noon on a November day. I was homeless. I was off the drugs, feeling better and on my way to starting new. I went to my mother's and asked if I could stay. Her answer was "Absolutely not!" I landed up rooming with a few friends for about a month; I stayed clean and off the drugs. Shortly after, I went on welfare and with the monthly grant, got a place of my own.

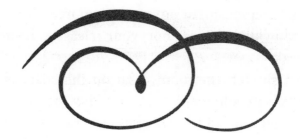

CHAPTER TWELVE

Witchcraft, Marriage, and Disaster

Sarah, a Practicing Witch

Sarah and I met at a local bar through mutual friends. I liked her right away. She mentioned that she was looking for someone to room with, so I invited her to come live with me. I was glad to have a friend.

We lived in an apartment building; on the top floor lived a drug dealer. Within weeks, I was back on the stuff. My new roommate was not into heavy drugs. She smoked a little pot, but she was dead against the hard stuff! However, she did not get on my case for doing them. Sarah had two things she liked to do: one, attend concerts to have sex with the band members, and two, practice witchcraft!

One day she opened up on the subject of witchcraft with me.

"That's a bunch of hocus pocus, Sarah."

"You think so, Carol? How about coming with me to Lily Dale?"

I had heard of the place; it was a Spiritualist Camp in Jamestown. I decided to take her up on the offer.

On a Saturday morning, Sarah and I took the two-hour

ride to the camp. When I passed through the gates, I marveled at the beauty of its location. It was sitting on a gorgeous piece of land in the valley. The grounds were covered with lush green grass and the landscape was filled with wild flowers.

Lily Dale is a self-contained village with its own grocery store, park and lake. It has a little hotel on the grounds and a big meeting hall. The people were very friendly and went out of their way to be nice to us.

Sarah planned to have a reading done by one of her favorite psychics, whose name was Luna.

"I cannot wait until you meet her, Carol; she is so right on and has great communications with the 'other side.'"

I have to admit I was looking forward to it.

Your Friend Has a Gift

Sarah had a one o'clock appointment. We were early, so a woman escorted us into the waiting room. I looked around the cluttered room. There were shelves loaded with books, and on the walls hung various pictures of fairies and angels. Near the window was a table with statues on it and votive candles burning.

At one o'clock sharp, the door opened. An attractive woman, who I guessed to be in her early forties, came in. She was dressed in a colorful floor-length dress. Her fingers were loaded with rings. She smiled at us and waved her arm in a gesture to come into her private chambers.

"So, Sarah, who is your friend?" she inquired. "I am feeling her vibration already." Her voice was as smooth as honey. She looked directly at me and asked, "Curious, aren't we?"

"Yes, curious and cautious," I replied.

Once inside, she and Sarah greeted each other with a

hug. I extended my hand to avoid the hug thing.

"Luna, this is Carol. We are roommates," Sarah explained.

"Tell me, Carol, what is it that you fear?"

I laughed nervously. "I have no fear, Luna, what are you referring to?"

She told me that my "vibration" gave her the distinct sense of fear.

"Is it the fear of the unknown or the fear of finding out that this is more than just an amusing afternoon?" she asked in her silky voice.

I was defensive. "Listen, I am not impressed with all this phony reading stuff."

She looked directly at me, her blue eyes piercing mine.

"Well, then let's do a reading on you and find out if it is phony, shall we?"

She led us to the reading room and pulled out a set of Tarot cards. She motioned for us to sit. The reading was officially in session.

Amazing and Accurate

By the time she finished, I was completely amazed. The things she told me, she had no way of knowing. I sensed a presence in the room. It was the same feeling I had when Marilyn visited me after her death. When it was over, Luna invited me to stay for tea. According to Sarah, this woman was impressed with me.

"You have gifts, Carol, and you should consider staying here for a while. We can teach you to exercise those gifts to benefit yourself and others. Do you believe in the other side?" she asked.

I did not answer her.

"That means you are not sure, correct? Well, then let me leave you with this: spirits are around you, Carol. You should find out why they are so near and tap into that realm. You would be amazed at the wisdom that these spirits have and that power is available to you!"

After our visit to Luna, Sarah insisted we stay for the evening session at the psychic-meeting hall. A man stood on the stage and called out names. People in the audience responded as he specifically named family members who had passed. He gave them messages from the deceased. I watched the people's reactions to his accuracy.

Just before he concluded, he approached me, pointed his finger and said, "You are about to embark on a journey that will change your way of thinking. Be open to the spirits and let them take you there."

Ouija, More Than a Game Board

After a day at the psychic camp, I decided to begin practicing the "craft." I could feel an invisible force around me, following the visit to the Spiritualist Camp. When Sarah got up in the morning, I was waiting for her at the kitchen table.

"I am ready for this," I told her.

"Good, let's get started tonight, after sunset."

That evening, Sarah came out of her room with an Ouija board.

"I wasn't talking about playing a game, Sarah."

She placed the board on the floor. "This board dates back to the Roman Empire; it's been around for centuries. At one time, it had all the signs of the zodiac and other markings on it. The pointer that spells out the messages used to be a writing device. As the messages came through, it wrote them out. The name *Ouija* is the combined words of yes, French and German." She squinted and glared at me. "I assure you, this is more than a game board."

The room was dark; Sarah lit a candle and put on some Celtic music.

"Let the games begin," I mocked.

We gently placed our fingers on the flat of the pointer. Sarah began asking questions. At first, there was nothing. Then slowly, the pointer began to cross the board.

"Stop that, Sarah, you are clearly moving it," I accused her.

The marker continued moving, spelling out words.

"I think this is all so silly," I said, getting up to leave.

"If you think that, Carol, then you go ahead and ask something I don't know the answer to. Go ahead."

I sat back down. I concentrated on a question. I knew there was no way Sarah knew the answer to this.

"Okay, let's see if this thing is for real," I said, placing my fingers back on the pointer with Sarah. It started moving erratically across the board, spelling out words and names at rapid speed. I was startled and removed my hand; Sarah looked over at me and lifted her hand. The pointer continued moving. I felt a change in the atmosphere. The room seemed darker and the air thicker. I felt something fill me. It was the most bizarre feeling. The candle blew out and Sarah's cat ran out of the room screeching. I could not move. The pointer had indeed answered my question. I was now convinced that I wanted to know this power and the sooner, the better.

The Beginning of My Journey

After that night, I was relentless. I wanted to know everything about the "occult." (I learned that the word *occult* means hidden.) I did not want anything hidden from me. I wanted to know all there was to know about this "other realm" and how it worked. I started collecting books on witchcraft, sorcery and divination. I studied card reading, psychics and incantations. I sought out all the top "witches" in the country. I studied the infamous Alex Crowley, a celebrated warlock. I was surprised when I discovered he was a heroin addict. I studied Edgar Casey and the lost continent of Atlantis. I looked into spell casting and meditations. I wanted to know all about the occult, solstices, and the special days like Halloween. I began a deep research on mythology and ancient pagan beliefs. I could never get enough information. I read up on Valid the Impaler, who was known as Dracula. I wanted to know about vampirism and get inside the mind of one who would feast on human blood. I found myself most interested in "spirit possession," as I felt these spirits could assist me on my journey and give me wisdom and power. I locked myself away reading and studying for months.

Finally, I was done. It was time to put all that I had gathered and learned into action and I was about to get my first crack at it.

Richard

Sarah and I were hanging out at a bar in town called Gilligan's. Buffalo's hot spot, it featured live bands on the weekends. We were standing around, sipping drinks and listening to the music, when I noticed a guy sitting on a bench against the wall. I nudged Sarah.

"Look at that guy over there! Wow!"

Sarah looked to where I was pointing and chuckled. "I know him, that's Richard. We dated for a while, nothing serious though. Do you want me to introduce you?"

I grabbed my lip-gloss, greased up my kissers and said, "Lead the way."

We walked over; Sarah stood directly in front of Richard, deliberately blocking the view.

He looked up. "Hey Sarah!" His voice was low and sexy. "How are you doing? I haven't seen you in a long time!"

She sat down next to him and started yapping away.

Well, so much for an introduction! Um, excuse me, did you forget why we came over?

I cleared my throat to drop the hint. "Ahem..."

Sarah stood up and put her arm around my shoulder. "Richard, this is Carol and she thinks you're hot."

My face turned three shades of red. I wanted to kill her!

He seemed unmoved by her blunt remark. Actually, he barely acknowledged me and continued to talk with Sarah. His friend Brian, on the other hand, was glad to make my acquaintance, but I wasn't having it; I had my sights on Richard.

Finally, I got up and announced I was going to the john.

"Aren't you coming with me, Sarah?"

She looked up and caught my angry look. "Oh yeah, sure, we'll be right back."

So off we went; I reamed her all the way to the bathroom. "What's your deal? I asked you to introduce me to Richard. Are you experiencing a brain fart?"

She apologized and assured me she would fix me up with him.

No Response

When we returned, Sarah sat next to Brian and started talking to him. I sat next to Richard; he did not seem pleased with the new seating arrangement. As he watched the band, I was sneaking glimpses of him. He was gorgeous, with hazel eyes, high cheekbones and a head of thick wavy hair. He was tall and lean. I caught a whiff of his cologne; I was intoxicated by the scent.

Holy smoke was I smitten!

I tried to open up a conversation but he was not contributing much. I figured he was disappointed that Sarah was now making out with his friend.

After about an hour, he stood up and said, "Hey Brian, I got to go; I have to work in the morning."

Brian wanted to stay, but Richard reminded him that there was only one ride home and it was about to leave! I grabbed a napkin off one of the tables, jotted down my number and handed it to him.

"Give me a call sometime if you like."

He looked down at the napkin, shoved it in his coat pocket and mumbled, "Yeah, sure." He took off out the door.

"He's a strange guy, Carol. Don't get your hopes up; he probably won't call you," Sarah warned me.

She was spot on; he didn't.

Can't Get Him Out of My Head

For some crazy reason, I could not get this guy out of my head. I could usually get any guy I wanted, but Richard was not interested—not one bit, and that got my goat.

The following week, Sarah and I went back to Gilligan's.

To my utter disappointment, he was not there, nor was his friend Brian.

"Give it up, Carol," Sarah told me. "There are a lot of cute guys here tonight that are interested in you. Why Richard?"

The fact is I did not want any other guy. I wanted Richard! I asked Sarah if she knew how to get in touch with him.

"I remember his last name, it's Kornacki. I think he lives in Lancaster with his parents, and he works for his father, who owns a construction company."

She grabbed the phone book and leafed through it. "Here it is; I got it!"

She dialed the number while I stood over her, anxiously waiting for a signal that he was on the phone. He was not home. Sarah tried at least five times, with no luck.

Let's Just Go There

"I have an idea; let's take a ride over to Richard's house and surprise him," Sarah suggested.

"You think he will mind?" I asked.

"Who cares? You're gaga over this guy, Carol," she laughed, "let's just do it!"

So we did.

We knocked on the front door. A nice-looking older man opened it. It was obviously his father.

He smiled at us and asked, "Can I help you?"

We told him we were there to see Richard.

"Oh Richard," he called out, "you have some very nice company."

He let us in and sent us down to the basement. When

Richard saw us, he was not happy. Apparently, he did not like surprise visits! Sarah told him to relax and take a ride with us to smoke some good pot. He agreed. In a short time, we were all laughing and having a good time. Still, his focus seemed to be on Sarah. When we dropped him off, our eyes met as he was getting out of the van, and my heart skipped a beat. He bid us a good night and went inside.

I was melting all over the front seat. "He takes my breath away!" I squealed.

I Will Use Witchcraft

Still, Richard did not call me or show up at Gilligan's.

Thus, I came up with a plan, one I was sure would work. I would use an incantation to stir his interest in me. I planned to use candle magic. I chose a certain day of the week, around midnight, to begin my ritual. I had gotten two pink candles, the color used for romance. They could not be large candles; I used tall, thin tapers. It was crucial that they were virgin, never used before. I believed in vibration and its power in this, so I was very particular. I took a piece of pink paper and wrote my desire upon it. Then I lit the candle, chanting my desire the whole time, calling on deities to empower my request. I ignited the paper with the candle flame, and as it burned, I chanted the same thing repeatedly:

Richard, you want me, no one else. You are obsessed with coming to me. You cannot think of anything else. Come, Richard, come.

As I watched the flame engulf the paper with my spell written on it, I pictured in my imagination him being near me and wanting only me. I let the candle burn through the night, however, I made sure no gust of wind or moving air would extinguish it. Each hour, I continued my repetitious chant, until the candle was burnt to a nub and gone. I kept the picture in my mind and refused to be moved. The incantation would bring him, I had no doubt.

It Worked

Eight days later, there was a knock on the door. Sarah answered it and I heard her greet the visitor.

"Well, hello there, Richard. Come on in."

"Is Carol here?" he asked.

I came walking out.

When Richard saw me, his face lit up. "Carol, can we talk?"

Sarah took off into the bedroom; she had a wicked smile on her face.

Richard and I sat down at the kitchen table.

"I can't explain this, Carol. This morning when I got up, all I could think about was you. I felt driven to come here as soon as I got off work. I have been obsessed with it. Do you think I'm crazy?"

I could hear Sarah giggling in her room. She knew the incantation had worked. She was not surprised!

One week later, Richard moved in permanently!

La Vida Loco – The Crazy Life

Richard's father was making the long trip from Lancaster to Buffalo every morning to pick him up for work because Richard did not own a car. Therefore, we decided to move closer to his job. We found an apartment in the town of Lancaster, just a short distance from his parents' house.

Within months, our place had a reputation. Every addict in town was hanging out with us. The police were at our door constantly. The tenants complained about the loud music and fights. Things often got a little crazy, and more than once, the night ended with broken bones. On two occasions, girls left with broken jaws; one had been punched in the face by her boyfriend, the other fell over a rail when she was too stoned to walk. I broke my leg, and one of our friends fell off a two-story roof, completely crushing the bones on his left side.

It was a time of injury, suicide and death. People were taking their lives in the craziest ways. One guy, who was suffering from depression, drove to the Peace Bridge and jumped off into the freezing Niagara River in the dead of winter. They found him four months later in the Horseshoe Falls; his body was so decomposed they could not identify him except for a tattoo. Another one of our friends was busted for possession of drugs. He freaked out in the jail cell and hung himself; he was seventeen years old.

Dirty needles, cotton fever, overdoses and bad drugs were all too common, and Hep C was being passed around by the infected ones. People were convulsing, while others were rushed to hospitals, only to die from an overdose upon arrival. Richard and I were totally whacked out. He was missing work because we stayed high all night and slept all day. The word on the streets was that the apartment was about to be raided and several arrests were going down!

Elizabeth, Richard's Mother

The first time Elizabeth laid eyes on me, disgust was written all over her face. What was her son doing with this alley cat? Richard had come from a refined and cultured family. He was smart and gifted, and she was optimistic about his future. To her, I was some sort of an insect that needed to be squashed under her feet. However, it quickly became apparent to her that her son was madly in love with this cheap and tawdry girl. For that reason, she decided to be nice to me, in order to keep her son close.

Mrs. Elizabeth Kornacki was stunning. She had fabulous taste in clothes and dressed in the latest fashions. Her home looked like a show place and she kept it immaculate. The woman was like a lioness with her four children. She was aware of their every move and worked hard at controlling their lives.

Mr. Kornacki was a gifted stonemason. It was his dream that his boys (Richard being the oldest) would one day run the company he had built from the ground up and retain its impeccable reputation.

Now, I had come along and invaded their son's life. It was apparent Richard did not intend to let me go. So how do you fight that?

Elizabeth decided that trying to change her son's mind was impossible. Therefore, she would do the next best thing; she would change me, or she would try, and that would be a great undertaking. I was common, uneducated, and—well, let us put it this way—I needed a lot of work! I dressed like a streetwalker, my make-up was overdone, I had no taste in clothes, and I had a filthy mouth. I would be a challenge, but Elizabeth was eager and willing to take me on.

A Mother's Plan to Save Her Son

Richard's mother was aware that time was running out

for us. The apartment in Lancaster was being watched and about to be raided. She knew the detectives in town and they informed her that they were intending to make a bust. When she tried to warn Richard, he denied that we were doing drugs.

I woke up one morning with excruciating pain on my right side. I was rushed to the hospital and admitted on the spot. I was diagnosed with gallbladder disease, in an advanced state. The doctor decided I needed surgery because the gallbladder was packed with stones.

After the surgery, complications set in, so my stay in the hospital had to be extended.

Back at the apartment, Richard was keeping up with the wild living.

In the meantime, Elizabeth was executing her plan to save her son from going to jail. The day I was released from the hospital, she drove Richard out to pick me up. On the ride home, we noticed that she was not headed toward our apartment in Lancaster.

Richard questioned her, "Where are we going, Mother?"

"You will see; I want it to be a surprise," she answered, with a hint of glee in her voice.

As we drove along, I was enjoying the view. The countryside was lovely. It was October and the trees were bursting with color. The cornfields had long given up their produce. The fall flowers were everywhere and pumpkins lay in the field, waiting to be harvested.

She pulled up the driveway of a beautiful house and pointed up at an apartment over the garage. Richard seemed annoyed with all the mystery.

"What the hell is this?"

"You'll see, my son; follow me."

We followed her up the stairs and when she put a key in the door, we began to get the picture. She pushed the door open and invited us to come in. What I saw inside astounded me. Every room was decorated with the "Elizabeth touch." There were gorgeous curtains, rugs, and fancy decorations on shelves, along with classy wall hangings. To be honest, I was thrilled. Richard, on the other hand, was not so happy.

"What is all this about, Mother? It appears you took it upon yourself to decide where Carol and I should live. Well, you wasted a lot of money and effort. We are going to continue to live in Lancaster, whether you like it or not."

"You don't live at the other place anymore," Elizabeth explained. "You have been evicted. I had your things moved here this morning while we were picking up Carol from the hospital."

"You did what? What gives you the right to decide our life, Mother?" He was fuming.

As they continued to argue, I walked from room to room, looking at all the fine furnishings. I came back into the kitchen, where they were still going at it hot and heavy.

"Richard, I like it here; it's so pretty."

He looked shocked. "You approve of what she did?"

I smiled and responded, "Yes, I do. Your mother put a lot into this. It is very nice. I would like to live here."

"You really like it, Carol?" Elizabeth asked.

"Yes, I do. I really do."

There is One Catch

The next morning, bright and early, Elizabeth showed up.

"You're not mad at me anymore, are you, Richard? I

wanted to do something nice for you and Carol; you understand, right?"

Richard gave her a hug. "No, I am not mad. Thanks, Mom, it is nice and Carol loves it."

"Good, I am glad. But there is one hitch: the landlord will not rent to a couple unless they are married, and I already told him you are."

"Was this your plan, Mother? To get us married?" Richard asked, his temper rising.

"It is my plan to get you on the right track, son. I am your mother and I know what is best for you," she replied, patting him on the back.

And so it was, Richard and I were to be married. We did not say much about it; we just let his mother make all the plans.

Our Wedding Day

When Elizabeth decided on something, there was no stopping her. She planned a small but elegant affair. We would be married at the Lancaster Town Hall by the justice of the peace. Afterwards, the wedding dinner would be held at her house. She decided the dinner menu, picked out the cake and invited the guests.

For my bridal dress, I chose a long, clingy knit gown in bright orange. When Elizabeth saw it, she was speechless.

"Carol, I will buy you any *white* suit or dress you want; price is no problem."

"Me wear white? Are you kidding? No, this will do fine. I like orange."

She gave in, but she was not happy with my choice. As for Richard, she made it a point to buy him the most expensive suit on the rack. He loved her taste in clothes, so he did not complain.

Our bridal party consisted of one person: Susie. She was a friend of ours who had a major crush on Richard. Why I chose her, I do not know. I guess she was the only one who could afford a dress.

I do not remember a single word we said at the "ceremony." We mumbled something and got the paper signed; then we were off to Elizabeth's house for the wedding supper. The table she prepared for us was beautiful. The gifts were wrapped with silver and gold ribbon. She had spared no cost. The cake was stunning and the food was fabulous. In the center of the table was an enormous bottle of imported Greek wine. The stuff was potent! We downed the entire bottle, mixing it with the drugs we had purchased for our "special day."

The Honeymoon Night … Fight!

Around midnight, everyone started to leave. His father did the honors and drove us to the apartment for our first night as man and wife.

On the way home, an argument broke out. I accused Richard of cheating on me with Susie before the wedding. He denied it vehemently, of course. By the time we got to the apartment, we were hitting each other over the head with the wedding gifts. When we got inside, all hell broke loose. He started name-calling, so I picked up a portable electric heater and threw it at him, missing his head by inches; it lodged in the wall, just above the baseboard. He opened the cabinet and threw all my favorite glasses on the floor, breaking them into a thousand little pieces. He smashed things against the wall and then started turning over the living room furniture. I stormed into his closet and began pulling out his clothes and tearing them up, then tossing them out the second-story window. We screamed obscenities and threatened to divorce in the morning. After about an hour of that, we were exhausted; we smoked some dope and then collapsed in bed.

In the morning, I heard a gentle knocking at the door. I dragged myself to the door and swung it open. There stood my father-in-law; he was holding a box of fresh warm donuts.

"Good morning," he chirped, "how are the newlyweds on their first day as a married couple?" He stepped inside and looked around at the room. He was horrified. Things were broken, smashed and turned over.

"Is everything okay here?" he asked in a shaky voice.

"Oh, yes," I assured him, "everything is fine."

He was staring at the heater that was lodged in the wall. I walked over and yanked it out; it left a large gaping hole. The man shook his head, handed me the box of donuts and left. I took one whiff of them and ran for the toilet, where I puked up wine for the remainder of the day. *So much for marital bliss!*

CHAPTER THIRTEEN

Coming Unglued

A Tender Moment

*I*t was our second-year anniversary. (The first two years were a blur. I wasn't sure if the marriage was going to survive.) I woke to the sound of music; it was coming from the living room. I walked in and found Richard sitting on the couch; he appeared to be deep in thought. When he saw me, he motioned for me to come and sit next to him. I did.

"Carol," his voice was hoarse, "I have been out here a long time, and I've been thinking. We both agree that we never intended to get married. We were lovers, but we didn't plan on making it legal; that was my mother's doing." He paused, as if to collect his thoughts. "I really do want to make this marriage work." He took my hand, "Listen, let's get off the drugs; they're destroying us. We can make a fresh start. What do you say? Want to make a go of it?"

I never expected him to come up with this. As for the drugs, I needed them, and I knew he did too. Besides, we didn't know any other way. We met stoned, lived together stoned, and now we were married … stoned. I wasn't sure if I could commit to do what he was proposing.

He stood up and guided me to the bedroom. We lay down together, and then he took me into his arms.

"Carol, as I sat thinking about you, about us, I realized that I truly love you and always will." His lips touched mine; they were soft and tender. He stroked my hair with his fingers and kissed my neck and shoulders. "I love you so much, Carol. I want us to make this work. Let's try."

He pulled my body against his. I melted into his arms and surrendered to his love. We made love through the night, but it was different. It was not *just* sex; we made love like husband and wife and it was blissful!

Afterwards, I held onto my husband's warm body. I could feel his heart beating close to mine. "I love you, Richard," I whispered breathlessly in his ear. I ran my fingers over his soft lips; they were still moist from our kiss. I looked into his beautiful hazel eyes and asked, "Richard, how can two people, who *love* each other so much, *hurt* each other the way we do?"

He pulled me closer. "I don't know, Carol, let's not talk about it. Just let me hold you!"

Rediscovering Each Other

Yes, there was madness in our marriage and at times, we lived as if the other did not exist. Then, in the midst of all the crazies, without rhyme or reason, the "dark clouds" would suddenly part and Richard and I would find each other again! It was a time when we rediscovered a love that was deep and passionate, a love neither of us could explain.

To escape any distractions, we locked ourselves in the apartment for days, refusing to answer the phone or the door. When we did venture out, it was to a nearby creek.

With our basket of fresh fruit, wine, cheese and a blanket to lie on, we strolled, hand-in-hand, down the path to our secret place. My husband filled my arms with wild flowers that he picked along the way. At our favorite spot, I spread out the blanket and opened the basket of goodies. Richard collected twigs and small branches for an evening fire.

Later, as the twigs crackled on the hot fire, we lay beneath the stars, pointing out constellations and sipping wine from paper cups. As we listened to the sound of the water cascading over the rocks in the creek and the wind rustling in the trees, we held each other tight. Sometimes our peaceful surroundings would lull us to sleep. Wrapped in each other's arms, we drifted off like there was no tomorrow.

The Big Announcement

When I missed my period, I was not surprised. I visited my OB/GYN and he confirmed that I was almost three months pregnant. I planned an intimate evening and created an atmosphere of love to announce the good news. We were in one of our "get clean and live right" modes, so I was sure Richard would be elated about the baby.

After a nice dinner, we were lying in bed and watching a movie. I reached over, took the remote and turned down the volume.

"Hey, what are you doing? I'm watching that," Richard complained.

I placed the remote on the table next to the bed and turned around to face him. "I have something to tell you." I took a long deep breath, "Okay, here it is: We are going to have a baby. I'm three months pregnant! Isn't that cool?"

He had a blank look on his face. "You are kidding, right?"

His response was like ice water thrown in my face. "No, Richard, I am not kidding. It's true! I am carrying our child."

He jumped up out of the bed. I followed him into the kitchen. He opened the fridge, grabbed a beer and popped it open.

"What's wrong? I thought you would be happy."

He rubbed his face in frustration. "I am far from happy, Carol. I don't want a kid—not now, not ever!"

"What are you saying? Do you want me to get an abortion, because that is not an option. I have already had two and I am not doing that again—ever!"

"Well, I suggest you rethink that because I am not having a kid."

I started to beg, "Please, honey, we can change our lives, get clean for sure this time and live decently as parents!"

There was no talking to him. He stormed out into the dark night. His last words were "I won't be a father."

You Can Have Other Babies, Just Not This One

The next morning, I paid a visit to his mom. Richard had been there the night before and told her the same thing he told me: "No baby!"

She tried to make me understand how "her son" felt.

"Listen, Carol, both of you are using drugs; don't think I don't know about it. Besides, you can have other children—later. My son just doesn't want a baby now."

She placed a couple hundred dollars in my hand, which she had docked from Richard's pay, and sent me off to the medical building in downtown Buffalo. "It's for the better," she told me as she walked me to the door.

I Love You, Little Baby, But You Must Die

When I arrived at the clinic, I walked upstairs and signed in. After what seemed like hours, I heard the woman call my name. I was led to a back office and questioned about the pregnancy. I handed her proof from the doctor. Then I was escorted to a small cubicle to change for the procedure.

I took off my clothes and put on a blue paper smock. I stood in front of the mirror staring at myself. I pulled the smock back, revealing my already rounded belly. I rubbed it gently. Inside, a child—Richard's baby!—was growing and being nourished in my body. As I stood there examining my abdomen, I began to weep.

"Little baby," I whispered. "My little baby, I love you and want you, but no one else does, so you have to die."

I released the smock and rubbed my tear-stained face. *Oh well, here we go again*, I thought. I walked out of the cubicle to the area where I would have the "procedure." I climbed up on the table, placed my feet in the stirrups and tried to relax. My mind traveled back to the old woman with the dirty hands and rubber tube. I had flashbacks of the second abortion in the sterile hospital where they gave me the D and C. I closed my eyes and waited for it to be over. I was trembling.

A doctor entered the room. He told me to relax, that it would be over quickly.

"The Procedure"

He turned on a machine that sounded like a vacuum. I heard a humming and felt a tug inside. It only hurt for a moment, and then he turned off the machine. He left the room quickly. The nurse helped me up and took me to another room, where I lay on a cot for about forty-five minutes. I was then released to go home.

Richard was not there to pick me up. A friend of the family showed up and drove me to our apartment. I walked up the stairs and went inside. I crawled on the bed and sat there gazing out the big picture window at the cornfields across the road. I was alone, very alone.

I thought I heard someone screaming; it was a deep throaty wail. Then I realized it was *me*! I started pulling out my hair, screaming wildly. I was coming apart. I looked around the room for an object to harm myself. I spotted my metal-tipped hairbrush. I picked it up and began hitting myself in the neck, dragging it down my skin, leaving deep scratches.

The Gun

I went into Richard's closet, where he kept a revolver. I began rummaging through his things, searching frantically for the gun. Finally, I found it. I checked the chamber for a bullet; there were three. I leaned back against the wall, cradling the gun in my hands.

"Richard," I cried in agony, "why? It was our little baby, yours and mine, our love child. Why didn't you want it? Why did you make me kill our baby?"

I pressed the gun against my neck and held it in position. *Let him find me like this; he will see what this has done to me.* I sat there, my finger on the trigger. Then I repositioned it; I put it in my mouth. The taste of the gunmetal stung my lips. I held it there, trying to get up the courage to press the trigger and end my life. My eyes darted wildly around the room.

"Do it!" I screamed with the gun jammed in my mouth. "Press the trigger!"

Everything was blurring; my mind was racing. In a rage, I took the pistol and threw it across the room. I held my head in my hands, cursing myself for being a coward and not ending my life.

When Richard came home from work that evening, I was completely out of it. I had gotten drugs and a needle to inject them. He said nothing of my afternoon at the abortion clinic and never mentioned the baby. We fell asleep in separate rooms.

We stayed married, but something died that day besides our baby. I was empty, unable to love or cope, and clearly unable to forgive him.

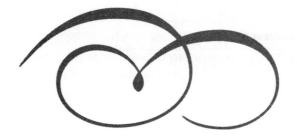

Chapter Fourteen

The Forbidden Visit

I Find My Daughter!

*I*t had been years since I had laid eyes on my daughter, Marilynn. I did not know where she was living; that information was kept from me by the court. Then something happened that changed all that.

While sitting at a bar late one night, a friend of a friend came up and sat beside me.

"Hey, Carol, how the heck are you?"

I raised my glass and nodded in response.

"Listen, I heard your kid is living in Sloan."

"How do you know that?" I asked.

"I work with a guy that lives across the street from the couple. He knows them and says they are nice people. It's the last house on Atlantic Street, a light brick duplex."

After giving me the information, he slipped his arm around me. "So tell me," he said, "how are you going to reward me for this valuable information?"

I pushed his hand off me and told the bartender to give him a drink on me.

My mind was racing. *My daughter is in Sloan! That is*

only fifteen minutes from where I am sitting! Is she really that close? I cannot believe it!

When I told my friend Anne, that I found out where my daughter was, she agreed to take me out there and check it out. The next afternoon, we headed to Sloan.

On the ride there, Anne reminded me not to make any trouble. I promised I wouldn't but I was a natural liar. I would do whatever prompted me at the moment, no matter what. And, if the opportunity presented itself, *I would snatch my kid and run!*

Anne drove by the house; it was very nice. It had large windows, a manicured lawn, flowers and a great big fenced-in yard with a swing set. On the front patio, toys were scattered about.

"Those must be Marilynn's," I said as she passed the house.

We drove by once, then stopped and parked a short distance up the street. Just then, I spotted a school bus coming around the corner. I knew Marilynn had to be in school; she was six years old. I wondered if she might be on that bus.

Anne reached over and patted my knee. "Settle down, let's just sit here and watch."

The bright yellow bus stopped at the corner. The doors opened and a little boy descended the steps. Then another child stepped off, a little girl with short brown hair. Her head was down and I could not see her face. When she looked up, I saw her eyes—those big, luminous brown eyes. It was my Marilynn! I felt my heart skip a beat. She was wearing a blue dress and carrying a little tote bag.

"There she is," I whispered.

"She certainly does resemble you, Carol," Anne said, "same big brown eyes."

Marilynn is Mine

I put my hand on the door handle and gripped it tightly; slowly, I began to lift it.

"Don't do that," my girlfriend cautioned.

"I have to, you don't understand," I argued.

"I understand more than you know, Carol. I have a child of my own, but this will only lead to trouble. Please don't."

Suddenly, a woman came out of the house; she went over to Marilynn and took her hand. Together they walked into the house; the door was shut behind them.

It was over; the brief moment that I got to see my little girl was over. I wanted to run up to the door and demand my child back. I wanted to scream, yell, and break something, anything to let the pain out of my heart.

"Marilynn is mine," I whispered. "That baby came out of me. I may be a bad mother, but even a bad mother loves her child!"

Anne knew this was breaking my heart. "I'm sorry, Carol. I will bring you back again, I promise."

She started the car. I pressed my hand against the window toward the house as the car moved further and further away.

"You will bring me back, Anne?" I asked, my voice cracking.

"Of course I will. You can count on it!"

The Promise Kept, a Stolen Moment

Anne kept her word; a few weeks later, on a warm summer day, she picked me up and headed back to the house where Marilynn lived.

We lucked out. She was in the backyard playing. Anne

suggested we park on the next street and cut through the yards to get closer.

"Now listen, I will do this if you give me your word you won't do anything crazy. Is it a deal?"

I gave her my word. I would just look and that was it.

We walked behind one of the houses and stood by the chain-link fence. I had a clear view of my daughter. Marilynn was on a swing, humming and singing to herself. She was alone.

Anne was nervous because we were standing in someone's yard. But there were no cars in the driveway and it was a Saturday afternoon. Still, she was uncomfortable being there.

As for me, I was a million miles away, watching my little girl as she played. Memories lit up corners of my mind: the first time I felt her kick inside my belly, and the pride I felt as a young mother when my little newborn baby was placed in my arms.

Grab My Baby and Run

Suddenly, Marilynn stopped swinging. She was watching us watch her. She slid off the swing and walked toward us.

"Hello, what are you doing in Miss Laura's yard?"

Anne stepped back and said, "Come on, we better leave."

Marilynn moved closer; now she was within reach. All I could think of was grab her and take off. The fence was not high and I could easily lift her over it. The car was parked on the street just steps away, the perfect "getaway."

Anne was aware of my spontaneity. "Don't do anything crazy," she cautioned me.

"Marilynn, come on in, lunch is ready," a voice was calling from inside the house.

I reached over the fence and gently touched her hair; she backed up.

"It's okay, honey, don't be afraid," I cooed.

Marilynn seemed transfixed. I now had a hold of her; this was the moment. All I had to do was lift her up over the fence and she would be mine.

"Don't do it, this is not the right time," Anne pleaded.

The voice from the house was persistent. "Marilynn, your lunch is getting cold. Come on now."

Marilynn turned and ran toward the house. Anne pulled me toward the car.

I Give Up

We got into the car and Anne drove away.

My heart was breaking. The sight of my daughter was more than I could bear. When she was born, I made her a promise that I would take care of her and be the best mother, but instead I had abandoned her. In my tormented mind, I was sure I deserved to die, or at least to be hurt for all the things that I had done and not done.

When I got back home, I stood in front of a mirror and called myself every name in the book. Then, in a rage, I scraped the skin off my neck and arms with my nails. I was empty and lifeless. The searing pain from the deep scratches felt good. I could feel something, which was far better than not feeling anything at all.

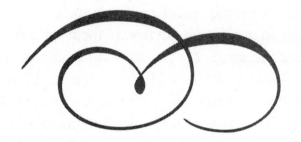

CHAPTER FIFTEEN

The "Ones Within"

More Spirits, More Power

I knew that I had to find a way to get Marilynn out of my mind, at least for a while. I was not getting her back, and to be honest, I knew in my heart that she did not need me as a mother. She was better off with me out of her life.

To distract myself, I got back into witchcraft. I found my niche in card reading. So, I focused on that. I was taking appointments for readings, and I was booking up fast. The "spirits" were keeping me informed of valid information during the readings. In an effort to expand my horizons, I decided to invite more spirits to inhabit me. To achieve this, I would have to go into deep meditation.

When the spirits appeared before me, they were beautiful. One was a female spirit; she looked like an Indian princess. A bright light surrounded her. She held in her left hand a small moon. I perceived her to be a spirit guide who could teach me the wisdom of the ancients. Another of them resembled an Egyptian man. He was tall and handsome. He held out his hands to me; in them were gold pins and a silver dagger.

Within five months, I had six guides. I referred to them

as the "ones within." Their presence increased my power. I could walk into a room and read people's mail, telling them secret things about their lives. Many were intrigued with my power; others feared me. I loved the attention.

One warm summer day in June, Richard and I took a ride to Lily Dale, the Spiritualist Camp. I wanted to pay a visit to Luna. This time I was not a skeptic. I was a believer! When we arrived, Luna was delighted to see me. I bubbled over with excitement as I informed her how this "new power" was working inside of me. She was not surprised.

"I told you, Carol, you have gifts. Now you are seeing and experiencing their power."

After our visit, I felt even greater empowerment.

Complete Surrender!

On Halloween night, a powerful spirit visited me. His presence made the hair on my arms stand up.

"Do you want some of this power, or do you want all?" he asked.

"What is the cost? Everything has a price ... what will I pay for it?"

"How much is your soul worth?"

I did not respond.

He repeated the question. *"How much is your soul worth?"*

"Is that the cost?" I asked, my voice quivering.

"Yes" was the response.

"And, in exchange for my soul?"

"More power than you ever imagined!"

I boldly entered in and agreed to the terms. Within moments of my decision, I felt transformed.

I was fearless.

Astral Projection, the Experience

I began to experiment with astral projection. I found that yielding my will made the experience easier. I had two adventures: one was unique, but the other scared me to death!

One morning after Richard had left for work, I sat on the living room floor in deep meditation. I was in touch with the "ones within." Suddenly, without warning, I felt a strange sensation; the next thing I knew I was looking down at my body. In total amazement, I watched as my soul floated above it. It was a feeling of complete freedom from the flesh.

I had read about Buddhist monks who would break free of their flesh by extreme fasting and meditation. They would have what they call "blood flashes," during which they were able to predict the future accurately. They too would have out-of-body experiences.

I was surprised how weak and sick my body looked as I moved about the room effortlessly. I sensed a need to return; when I thought it, I was back in.

I tried to share what happened with Richard when he got home. He burst out laughing. "You sound like a lunatic. I suggest you quit that stuff; it's getting the best of you, Miss Pagan Witch."

A Fight to Get Back In

A few weeks later, I had another experience, one that was quite different. This time I was in a van. We were on our way to meet with some people who were studying Eastern religion. I was expanding my knowledge and spending a lot of time with them.

On the way to the meeting, I decided to meditate. Suddenly, I was out of my body. I looked down and saw the driver inside the van and myself in the back seat in a lotus position. I was fascinated as my soul traveled effortlessly above the vehicle, at the same speed. It was the most freeing feeling—incredible! After a few minutes, I attempted re-entry. However, I could not get back in. I struggled, but was unsuccessful! I could see my body inside the moving vehicle. I looked pale and slumped over in a weird position. I was starting to panic. I exerted every ounce of my willpower to get back. Then suddenly, I returned; my body shook violently on the re-entry.

"Hey, Carol, you all right?" The driver looked concerned. "You were wigged out there for a while."

"I'm okay now," I assured him. But I really wasn't; the out-of-body experience scared me. That was the last time I messed with it.

Strange Behavior … Me or the "Ones Within"?

Late one night, Richard and I were lying on the bed talking. What happened next, I am not exactly sure. Nevertheless, I looked up to find Richard on top of me with my shoulders pinned down; there was a look of horror on his face.

"Let me go!" I screamed, pushing him off. "What's the matter with you, Richard? Are you crazy?"

He jumped up and backed away from me. "I'm not crazy, Carol; you're the one who is nuts! I think you are possessed or something. You just put a pillow over my head and tried to suffocate me!"

"That's a lie!" I yelled.

"It's not a lie, Carol. You began speaking in a strange voice; you sounded like a man. I thought you were fooling around. Then you grabbed the pillow and put it over my head." He slipped into his pants and headed for the door. "I think all this witchcraft stuff is getting out of hand!" He took off to the bar down the street to get a stiff drink.

I sat there trying to figure out what had happened. *Why can I not remember anything? Why was I unaware of it? Did I blackout? Was it I or the "ones within"?*

It troubled me for weeks. I could not let it go and continued to ponder over it. *Why the sudden switch? Have I stepped into an evil dimension? Have I been deceived? What have I done wrong?*

Surely, I was doing everything right. I was certain of it. I had the ability to cast spells, do incantations and predict people's futures with accuracy. I had several "spirit guides" that were giving me unlimited wisdom. I was faithful in my worship of the goddess and I did homage to Pan. I sought knowledge from mother earth and learned to hear the voice of the spirits. So what was the problem? What could I be missing?

I was becoming very concerned about this "violent act" against Richard (who, needless to say, had been sleeping with one eye open).

With the Power Comes Fear!

I was convinced that I did not need to join a coven or some secret society! I was a renegade witch who practiced by my own rules. I was not into midnight runs in the forest, hugging trees and having orgies. That was not my style!

I knew when I started this that there would be a price.

However, I did not think it would turn into this! Wasn't I supposed to be the one giving orders to the "ones within"?

I decided that I would dismiss them. I would not call on them for anything. I thought that was all it would take. I was about to find out it was not that easy. I made a deal with the devil when I lusted over this power, and I would be held to that agreement! I had sold my very soul and it was becoming painfully clear that there was no refund!

The further I tried to get away, the harder the "ones within" fought.

At times, even operating a car posed a problem. While I was driving, without warning the "ones within" would seize me. The steering wheel would begin to jerk wildly. Their voices were in my head, ordering me, "Just let it happen. You will die, but you will be reincarnated; this is your chance to be reborn." Fighting to gain control of the car, I hit the brakes and skidded into a guardrail.

After a few of those encounters, I realized the "ones within" were planning to kill me!

Mikki Returns

It was a hot, humid day in July. There was a knock at the door. I opened it; I recognized the guy, but I was too stoned to make out who the girls were.

They were looking for drugs. I let them in.

Then I heard a familiar voice. "Carol, aren't you going to say hi?"

"To whom?" I asked.

"To me," she replied.

I looked over; the sun was blinding my view. "Should I know you?"

She moved out of the glare and I got a clear picture. *It was Mikki!* I almost fell over. She looked different, very thin and gaunt. She was shaking. I knew that meant only one thing: she had come back from the city an addict!

I tried to give her a hug; she pulled back and glared at me.

"I am so happy to see you, Mikki! When did you get back to Buffalo?"

"Three months after you left me in New York, Carol."

I tried to explain about the Yonkers deal—how Billy had left me in the apartment building, and how I was forced to come home or face time in a detention center.

Mikki was not buying it!

"I'm not here for explanations; I need drugs. That's all I want from you and I will be gone."

I walked into the living room and lit a cigarette. "Mikki, you were hung up on Moses. I tried to get you to leave, *twice*, but you refused!"

She laughed. "So you just came home and forgot about me, is that it Carol?" She pulled some money out of her pocket. "I didn't come here for any of this bleeding-heart crap. I'm sick and I need something now!"

"So, you're hooked, Mikki?"

"Aren't you, Carol?"

"Yes, I am."

"Then that makes two of us."

After I gave Mikki the drugs, she asked me if she could use my bathroom to shoot them. I told her to go ahead.

A Pitiful Sight, and it's My Fault

Mikki had been in the bathroom for some time. I was starting to get concerned; had she overdosed in there? I pounded on the door—no answer. I pushed it open. There she was, slumped down next to the toilet, my young friend. The needle was still in her arm, filled with blood, and her mouth was gaping open. No, she was not dead; she was stoned out of her mind.

I was paralyzed with anguish and shame. Mikki and I had grown up together. How could I let this happen to her?

It was my idea to go to New York City. She was only eighteen years old. I should have protected her, and above all, I should not have left her there. Now she hated me, and I did not blame her one bit, because I hated myself more!

With Mikki back in Buffalo, there were times that we would run into each other at the local "shooting gallery." Most often, she avoided me and left right after she shot up. One day, I approached her and struck up a conversation.

"Hey Mikki, whatever happened to Moses, and how did you get home to Buffalo?"

"Moses was busted for possession of heroin in a subway station, so I called my mother and she flew me home," she replied coldly.

After we talked that day, I called her and we chatted some. I had hoped that if I was persistent enough, Mikki might soften up and we could rekindle our friendship. Just when I thought I was making headway, something occurred that made it painfully clear to me that Mikki *still* resented me for leaving her in New York City.

Take it All, You Junkie Pig

It happened one day when she and her boyfriend Mike

showed up at our door looking for heroin. I had some and decided to share it with them. I thought it might help Mikki and me to get close again.

Mike was administering the shots to Richard, Mikki, and me. When he was done, there was one shot left, and it was supposed to be his. I started complaining that I did not get enough. I wrapped the belt back around my arm and insisted he give it to me.

"Come on, Carol, don't do this, you had some; you said this was mine," he argued.

I grabbed his arm, insisting he give me the rest. "I paid for it, and it is *my* dope!" I screamed.

I always acted like this, even when I had enough. I was greedy when it came to dope and everyone knew it.

Mike started yelling and pushing me away. "You're a pig, Carol, a stinking pig. Enough is never enough for you. Okay, you want more, I'll give you lots more!"

He drew up the remainder of the heroin and wrapped the belt tightly around my upper arm. He pressed the needle into my flesh. He pushed down the plunger, emptying the heroin into my blood stream. Our eyes met; he had a smirk on his face, like a dark demon. A warm feeling rushed through my body—the morphine kick—and every muscle relaxed; I floated into a sweet euphoria.

Then something happened. My body went totally limp.

"Goodnight, piggy," Mike said as he grabbed his coat and headed for the door. "Come on, Mikki, let's get out of here, she deserves it."

I fell to the floor with a hard thump. The last thing I heard was Mikki's voice cry, "Oh my God, her lips are turning blue!" They were out the door in a flash!

Richard was freaking. "Come and help me with her, please!"

Mikki never looked back.

Richard was left to pull me out again! After a long, strenuous night of slapping me, walking me and plunging me in ice baths, I slowly made my way back, but just barely!

CHAPTER SIXTEEN

A Fresh Start?

I Am a Land Owner

Spring was in the air. Everything was coming up fresh. The barren branches were now budding green leaves. Flowers of every color were bursting through the moist ground. The rain filled the air with a clean scent and the birds that had been silent during the icy cold winter were now singing as the morning sun rose up into the crystal blue sky. Even with all this wonder and beauty surrounding us, Richard and I were very miserable!

The phone rang; it was my mother—surprise, surprise.

"Well, for you to call me, either someone died or I owe you; which one is it, Mom?"

"Don't be such a smart mouth; I'm your mother, show some respect."

I sighed, "What?"

"Your grandmother Bertha has contacted me through an attorney; she is about to divide the land in North Carolina. Since Dad is deceased, she will be giving his part to his heirs. We are expected to fly down there; do you want to go?"

I was silent. Hearing Grandma Bertha's name made my heart skip a beat.

"Are you there, Carol?"

"Yes, I am, and yes I will go with you. Who else is going?"

Mom informed me that my oldest brother, Ronnie, and two of my sisters, Kathy and Debbie, would be taking the trip with us.

I felt uncomfortable with the whole idea. I was the black sheep of the family and they had little to do with me. Besides, it had been a long time since I had seen any of my family. The only time I was around them was the holidays (if I chose to even show up), and more often than not, I was stoned and obnoxious.

"Well, what is it? Are you going to go with us?"

"Yes, I will go."

The trip was planned for April. We would fly out of Buffalo to Washington, where our layover was about four hours, and then on to North Carolina. My brother Ronnie made arrangements for us to sightsee while we were in Washington.

When the day in April finally arrived, we all met at my mother's house. The atmosphere was noticeably tense. Guess they thought I would show up stoned; I did, but not enough to worry about. At first, everyone was quiet, going through the motions at the airport and being seated on the plane. After the plane took off, we all had a few drinks. That loosened us up and we were beginning to have a nice time.

When we got off the plane in Washington, we were ready for our four-hour layover, with lots to do and see. The cherry pink and apple blossom white flowers filled the trees.

There were tulips and crocuses everywhere. It was spectacular. The White House, the Washington and Lincoln monuments, we visited them all! After a few hours, we were all laughing and getting along. I felt like part of the family again. Even Mom and I were being civil to each other—a major accomplishment!

The flight from Washington to North Carolina was very short. When we arrived, we rented a car.

"Your father's family doesn't like me, never has," Mom told us on the ride over to Grandma Bertha's house. "To them, I am a loud Yankee woman who ran her mentally ill husband out of his own home and had him committed to an institution!"

We all knew that Dad's illness was not anyone's fault; it just happened. After years of suffering and escaping the hospitals, he went home to North Carolina, where he later died of an aneurysm. A vein in his head burst; he died two days later. For this and a whole lot more, they resented Dorothy and she knew it. Yet, that did not stop her from getting what she considered rightfully hers, and that was her husband's land.

Reunited With My Precious Grandma Bertha

I had not seen Grandma Bertha in years. I was filled with excitement at the thought of being reunited with her.

When Mom walked in with us, the room grew quiet. She was greeted cordially, but it was obvious they hated her. I scanned the room for my Grandmother. Then I saw her; she was serving iced tea to the gathering. When she spotted me, a big smile came on her face. She opened her arms for me to come to her.

"My goodness, it has been so many years since I saw you, child; come and give your grandmother a hug."

I put my arms around her and laid my head on her shoulder. Now, at twenty-four years old, I was the one who was taller. I did not want to leave the peace and comfort of those loving arms. I basked in the sweet odor of her clothing and the sound of her voice saying my name.

Grandma Bertha gently pulled away and looked into my eyes. "Just like when you were a little girl, you loved those hugs; oh yes, I remember, you didn't want to let go."

Grandma moved on and greeted her guests. I sat down on the sofa and watched her every move. On the other side of the room, my mother sat quietly, watching the exchange between Grandma Bertha and me. I could not help but wonder what thoughts were going through her head. After all, she had kept me from my grandmother for so many years, but now she could not stop me.

Two days later, we boarded a plane to return to Buffalo. We were now landowners and clueless as to what we were going to do with it.

So, You Are Leaving Marilynn Behind?

Richard and I were in rough shape. Therefore, I suggested we move.

"To where?" he inquired.

"North Carolina. I have property there."

Richard chuckled, "North Carolina, are you serious?"

"Yes, we can get off the drugs and start a new life."

"We've tried that a number of times," he reminded me.

"Yes, but this will be different."

"I doubt it." His voice dripped with cynicism.

After our conversation, he left the house. Several hours later, I heard him come in.

"Okay, I am willing to try; the move will do us good. Besides, we need to look into that land you have inherited."

When we informed Richard's mother of our move, she was troubled. One day, unexpectedly, she stopped by.

"So, you're leaving your little girl behind, Carol?" she asked.

"If this is one of your sneaky ways of getting us not to move, you're wasting your time," Richard warned her.

"Marilynn is in good hands and she is happy; she doesn't even know that I exist," I answered in my defense.

"How do you know she's happy, Carol? Have you asked her?"

"I have been out to the house where she lives and from what I saw, she doesn't miss me or need me."

Elizabeth motioned me to sit down. I was hesitant, but I did.

"Carol, I can't imagine my child being raised by strangers. Do you miss your daughter?"

I rubbed my hands together nervously. "Of course I do, but the court has made a decision, and you know as well as I do that I am not a fit mother!"

Elizabeth argued the point. "You haven't even tried, Carol. Maybe it is time you do."

By the end of the afternoon, it was decided; we were going to get Marilynn back.

Elizabeth Does it All

We put our moving plans on hold and concentrated on getting my daughter back.

First, Elizabeth decorated a room for Marilynn and filled it with toys and games. She hung dainty curtains and bought her a bed and dresser set. Whenever the people from Child Welfare Services (CWS) came around, Elizabeth made her presence known and assured them that she would be willing to appear before the judge on my behalf, if necessary.

Finally, Marilynn was brought over to the house by the social worker, for her to observe us as mother and daughter. Marilynn was seven years old. When I tried to hug her, she recoiled. The fact is she did not want to be there. She cried, screamed, and resisted me on everything. I was exasperated! Elizabeth, on the other hand, managed to change all that. With her arms laden with toys and a gentle word, she won Marilynn over. She took her into the newly decorated room and sat playing with her for hours. If one thing was for certain, Marilynn and Elizabeth were hitting it off! Richard was cordial and nice, but he was "anti-kids" and it showed. As for me, I tried to pick up where I left off as a mother.

After several weeks of investigation by the state of New York, custody of Marilynn was handed over to me, with a strong warning and many rules. Elizabeth gave the CWS her word that Marilynn would receive the best care. The CWS rep made it clear that Elizabeth Kornacki's involvement and dedication to the case was what sealed it.

I was overjoyed! Marilynn was now in my custody! I was reinstated as her mother, and Richard would be her "father." I hoped that this would be a new beginning for us to be a happy family.

The Move to North Carolina

Richard, Marilynn and I were off to our new life as a

family in North Carolina. Grandma Bertha was still living in the old house where we used to visit her. She invited us to stay with her until we found a place of our own.

When we arrived, I got out of the car and ran into her arms.

"Sweet child, I thank God you are here!" she exclaimed.

Early the next morning, I was out of bed in a flash and in the kitchen to help her prepare breakfast. The joy I felt was indescribable. I dared to believe that maybe God had brought me there for a reason and I let that hope fill my heart. With the land I inherited, and Marilynn now with us, I was sure Richard and I could make a new life.

We lived with Grandma Bertha for about four weeks. My cousin Glover rented us a double-wide mobile home on his property near the river. He owned some businesses, so to help us out, he hired Richard to work for him.

We had little money and a broken-down car. However, we were optimistic. We planned to build on the property that I inherited and maybe start a business there.

Marilynn and I spent the hot summer days walking the beach, building sand castles, collecting shells and romping in the cool green water. I was learning to be a "mom" and Richard was turning out to be a good "dad."

We had a hard time at first not having the drugs to which we were accustomed. We both had some serious withdrawals, so we substituted the heavy drugs with pot and alcohol; even so, being off of the needle made us feel like we were doing better.

With Marilynn now my focus, I stayed clear of the "occult" practices. The "ones within" were silent, but I knew that they were still inside me and could surface at any time.

Another Clearing

The dark clouds that were constantly invading our marriage had parted again. This time, Richard and I were sure they were gone for good. Our days were filled with love and laughter; our nights, passion. We were husband and wife, mother and father, lovers and best friends. Finally, we had reached the unreachable. We had come to a place of peace within our marriage. It was too good to be true.

Richard and Marilynn got along quite well. He took special interest in her schoolwork and built a custom bed for her room. On the weekends, we drove up to the Smoky Mountains and camped out in tents. During the week, we strolled down to the river walk and watched the fishing boats, loaded with shrimp and fish, as they glided to the dock. We were now a family and we loved being together.

For two blissful years, we enjoyed life, marriage and Marilynn.

Another Big Announcement!

It was in the middle of a hot summer that I realized I had missed my period. My initial reaction was panic! *Could I be pregnant?*

Richard noticed the change in my demeanor and asked, "You're acting strange, what's wrong?"

I took a deep breath. "I think I might be pregnant."

He got a weird look on his face. "No way, you're not!"

I felt sick to my stomach. With a trembling voice I asked, "Are you going to send me for another abortion, Richard?"

He did not answer, just poured himself a stiff drink and downed it.

I took that as a bad sign. His parents were planning to come down for a visit, but now I was not so sure it was a good idea.

When they arrived, Richard was drunk and rude. I was very embarrassed! Over dinner, I broke the news about the possibility that I might be pregnant. Elizabeth was quiet; however, his father was elated.

"Well that's wonderful," my father-in-law replied as he got up to give me a hug.

"I don't mind Marilynn, but that is as close as I will ever get to being a father," Richard barked.

"You can't ask Carol to have an abortion again, son!" his father protested.

"Mind your own business," Richard said angrily.

"If I am to be a grandfather, then it is my business."

Richard got up from the table, mixed himself another drink and stormed out of the house. Elizabeth followed him. I jumped up and started clearing the table.

"Carol," my father-in-law's voice was tender, "I am sorry my son is acting like this, but don't worry, I am sure he will get used to the idea."

"I don't think he will ever get used to the idea, Dad," I told him, "he is afraid of responsibility and a baby requires that."

I ran into the bedroom and cried my eyes out. Things were tense after that. No one was sure how to act. Richard stayed drunk, while his mother babied him, and my father-in-law tried to keep everyone happy. It was a very difficult time.

Richard's Relief, My Disappointment

I woke up one morning with severe cramps. I ran to the bathroom; blood was gushing out of me. I held onto my midsection. It felt like fire was searing through my abdomen. Could this be my period, or was it a miscarriage of the child my husband didn't want? I pulled myself up off the bathroom floor and took a hot shower.

Over breakfast, I announced what had happened. Richard's sigh of relief was heard by all of us. If Elizabeth was saddened by the news, it certainly didn't show. On the other hand, his father had a sick look on his face, as if someone had just died. He quickly got up from the table and excused himself. I heard his car start and drive away.

The next day, after they left, I drove alone to the ocean. I sat on the cool sand, listening to the sound of the waves lapping the shore. Over my head, a blanket of stars glistened in the night sky. As I swept the hot tears off my cheeks, I thought about the cold attitude that my husband had displayed over the possibility of us having a child together. I was stricken with a sick realization that though he was my lover, husband and friend, I would never carry his child.

So, I went to the doctor and got put on birth control pills. After that, Richard and I began to drift apart; the magic we had shared in our marriage was fading. The nights of passion and love were washed away in a tidal wave of anguish and disappointment.

Back to Buffalo

After the pregnancy scare, it was one thing after another. Richard lost his job and started drinking even heavier, if that was possible; the guy was downing a quart of Jack Daniels pretty regularly. The rent was due, the bills were piling up and food was scarce. Besides that, we were fighting every day.

When Grandma Bertha died, I was devastated. Things being as they were between Richard and me made living together a total drag. We stayed clear of one another as much as was possible.

Finally, in complete frustration, I made a suggestion.

"Why don't we just go back to Buffalo?"

Richard agreed heartily.

So we packed up our meager belongings and headed back to our old stomping grounds: Buffalo, New York.

When we arrived, it was winter and freezing cold. We had to readjust to the weather, having lived in a warm southern climate for two years. My girlfriend let us move in with her on a "temporary basis." The winter weather made it impossible for Richard to find construction work. Thus, we found ourselves in the same situation: no job and no money.

I interviewed for a job at the Poets Lounge; I was hired on the spot. We found a small apartment that was literally falling apart. While I was at work, Richard was at home fixing the place up. When we were finished with the renovations, it was cozy and homey. But, try as we may, something was lost and I doubted we could ever get it back.

When I got off work late at night after the Lounge closed, I usually stuck around and partied. As for Richard, he found solace elsewhere. By spring of our first year back in Buffalo, we were back on the needle, worse than ever!

The apartment that we were renting happened to be just a few blocks from Marilynn's foster family. When Marilynn asked me if it was all right for her to go to their house, I agreed. Ordinarily, I would have blown a gasket, primarily because of jealousy, but considering the condition Richard and I were in, I knew she was better off over there. Besides, the environment the foster parents provided was stable and I could see it had a positive effect on her.

The Return of Beth

I woke up in a panic. It was the middle of the night and the room was pitch black. My body was covered in sweat and my heart was beating a mile a minute. Richard was out and Marilynn was spending the weekend with her foster family. Yet, I could feel a presence in the room; it hovered over me. It brushed past my face.

"Who are you and what do you want?" I asked aloud.

"It's Beth; I have come to relieve you of your miserable self, Carol."

"Leave me alone and go away; I don't want you occupying my mind. Do you understand?"

I could hear evil laughter fill the room. I pressed my hands to my ears to shut her out. I got out of the bed and paced the apartment. She continued to converse with me.

"So, have you missed me, Carol?"

"You're not real, Beth. You are a figment of my imagination and I can overcome you."

"I doubt that," she mocked.

I ran out to the backyard; she was there. I raced back into the apartment, trying to outrun her, but she was there. I covered my head with pillows; she was there. I felt like my mind was shredding into a thousand little pieces.

The "ones within" joined her as she continued to torment me.

I was huddled in the corner, clutching my pillow when I heard the apartment door open. There were footsteps coming toward me. A tall dark figure stood in the doorway; it loomed over me. I could barely breathe.

"Carol, what is your problem?"

It was Richard.

I crawled out of the corner and got into the bed. He stripped down and climbed in next to me. I fell asleep clutching his arm.

Free-Falling

To silence the voices of Beth and the "ones within," I increased my intake of drugs. I stayed stoned and sometimes did not get out of the bed for days. When I did go out, I did bizarre and dangerous things.

At a local bar one night, I mixed a bunch of pills with scotch. The person who was drinking with me suggested we take a walk. The air outside was hot and muggy. A few blocks from the bar was a school with a swimming pool on the property.

"Hey, Carol, want to go swimming?"

"Sure, sounds like a good way to cool off."

We climbed the five-foot fence and dived into the bath-like water, fully clothed. The pool was eight feet on the deep side. As I swam under water, I could see the lights above me. The drugs relaxed me … too much. Before I knew it, I was sinking to the bottom. I made no effort to surface. I was intrigued with the feeling of floating down. I knew I had to breathe and I was starting to struggle. I tried to move my legs in an effort to ascend, but they were not cooperating and I could not hold my breath any longer. *How am I going to reach the top of the water?*

After an enormous effort, I surfaced, gasping for air. I crawled out of the water and lay on the concrete beside the pool.

The guy came over and asked, "You all right, Carol?"

"Yeah sure," I replied. "I almost drowned just now; it was scary and fascinating at the same time."

He looked at me as if I was insane. "Well, we're soaked. I am going home; do you want a ride?"

"No, I think I will go back and get another drink," I told him.

"You're kidding, right? You're sopping wet; you can't go in there like that."

"Oh yes, I can. Watch me."

I walked back across the street to the bar; my wet hair was plastered to my face and I had raccoon eyes from my running mascara. I went directly to the bar and ordered a drink, leaving a trail of water behind me. I could hear people giggling and making fun of me, but I did not care. I just did not care!

CHAPTER SEVENTEEN

Give Me Death

Carol is Dying

*T*he hepatitis that I contracted in New York City was taking a toll on my liver. I was constantly sick. I landed up in the hospital a few times. The pain in my stomach was overwhelming, and even the large amount of drugs I was using did not stop the cramping.

My doctor ordered a series of liver tests. When he called the house with the results, I was out, so Richard took the call.

"Mr. Kornacki, your wife is seriously ill," he explained, "in fact, she may be dying! The biopsy that I performed on her liver shows the virus is progressing rapidly. I attribute this to her drug and alcohol addiction. I have repeatedly cautioned Carol about her drinking, but obviously, my warnings have fallen on deaf ears."

He continued to explain to Richard the severity of my condition. "Her liver enzymes are elevated, quite high, actually. Then there is the issue of the bleeding ulcers: Carol has two of them. We have located a rather large one in her duodenum—"

Richard interrupted, "So what are you going to do to help her?"

"The question is," the doctor retorted, "what is Carol going to do to help herself? I have tried and gotten very little cooperation from her. Your wife doesn't understand the seriousness of her failing health; personally, I think the woman has a death wish."

The doctor took a deep breath. "I am sorry, Mr. Kornacki, but I don't feel that I can continue to treat Carol. I have decided to release her as my patient. She deals with major anger issues and has a violent temper. On her last visit to my office, she threatened to harm my nurse and used profanity. My advice would be to get your wife some professional help as soon as possible!" The doctor sounded exasperated. "Do you have any questions, Mr. Kornacki?"

"No, not a thing," Richard said hotly, as he hung up the phone in the doctor's ear.

Carol, This is Serious

When I walked in the house late that night, my husband was waiting for me. I turned on the light and there he was. He took a long drag on his cigarette and threw it in the ashtray.

"Sit down, Carol; I have something to tell you." His voice was grim.

"Why so serious?" I inquired as I sat down across from him.

"I talked to Doctor Kline today; according to the test results, you are extremely ill," he paused, "possibly dying."

"You talked to him?"

"Well, of course I talked to him; I didn't just come up

with this stuff! He called this afternoon."

For the next half hour, Richard covered all the details of their conversation, including the doctor's decision to release me as a patient because of my behavior in his office. After he finished, we sat there staring at each other.

Finally, I jumped up. "Oh well," I said flippantly, "we all have to die sometime. Sounds like an escape hatch to me. This life sucks, so looks like I am checking out early."

I started walking out of the room then turned and faced him. I smiled wickedly and added, "Hey, think of it this way, Richard. I will be in hell a lot sooner than you!"

He looked flabbergasted. "Carol, do you realize how serious this is?"

"So what?" I said, acting as if I didn't have a care in the world. "Richard, I have held loaded guns in my mouth with my finger on the trigger, drove cars into telephone poles, and deliberately overdosed; and you find it surprising that I don't give a damn if I live or die? Where have you been for the last three years? On another planet?"

I think I detected a "very concerned" look on my husband's face. I am not sure—it had been so long since we were civil to each other. However, my guess is that he did not want me to die.

A Moment of Reflection

One summer afternoon, after sleeping most of the day, I woke up to find myself alone. I walked down the stairs and plopped down on the concrete porch. Above me, the sky was crystal blue. I watched as a big, fluffy white cloud moved slowly over my head. I glanced around at the unkempt yard; the lawn was overgrown with weeds and dandelions. In the back, on the old wooden fence, a pink rose bush had blossomed; the scent filled the air like sweet perfume. I walked over and touched one of the delicate petals. The grass felt good beneath my bare feet. I stood still, watching and listening to the sights and sounds of summer. Birds were chirping and singing. A stray cat disappeared under the house. Children wandered by, giggling and poking one another. A neighbor waved at me from across the street. In the distance, I heard the sound of lawnmowers and I could smell fresh cut grass. Yes, it was a lovely day.

The Worst Crime, a Wasted Life

I went to the mailbox, reached in and pulled out some envelopes along with a bunch of junk mail. I knew the envelopes were late notices, so I did not bother to open them. It had been a pleasant hour, and I did not want to botch it up with threats to turn off the electricity or gas. I headed back up the stairs. I threw the mail on the kitchen table and sat down on the couch.

Suddenly, I was overcome with a sense of dread and fear. *Okay, I am dying. Everyone dies; I already got that part. But this came unexpected. I have always planned my death to be by my own doing. This is out of my control. I have a terminal disease that is turning my liver into a piece of leather …*

As I sat there, I realized for the first time that I was totally out of control of my life and my death. I felt useless. Everyone would be better off—my kid and my husband. The marriage was in name only and we were ready to divorce. My daughter could go back to her foster family and avoid having me ruin the rest of her life. Then it dawned on me that I had not done one decent thing in my life, and now I was dying.

I heard Richard coming up the stairs. He walked in, passed me by and headed straight for the refrigerator.

"I'm hungry; I don't suppose you made anything to eat, did you?"

I picked myself up off the couch and went into the kitchen to get his dinner.

We ate in silence; I barely touched my food.

You Looking For a Miracle, Carol?

After dinner, I opened the subject.

"Linda Smith has invited us to attend one of the Friday-night meetings at her church; would you consider going, Richard?"

He looked over at me and chuckled, "You are kidding, right? You're not getting weird, are you, Carol?"

"*Getting weird*, Richard? Have you taken a good look at our lives? We are drug addicts; we fight constantly and neither of us has been faithful. You haven't had a stable income for months, and I can barely make it to work because I am so sick. We don't have any money and they are threatening to repossess the car. In addition, if that is not enough, I am a practicing witch that has blackouts and channels dangerous spirits! My conclusion, Richard, is I think we both arrived at 'weird' a long time ago!"

He was not sure if he should laugh or tell me off.

"Then you go, Carol; you're the one into all the hocus pocus."

He got up and disappeared into the bathroom. After a few minutes, he came out.

"Why are you suddenly interested in going to a religious meeting? Are you afraid of dying, Carol? Did that doctor's report scare you?"

"No!"

"Then it must be Linda; you seem to like her. Is she the reason you want to go? Has she promised you some sort of miracle?"

"Linda is very nice to me, Richard, and there are few who bother with me anymore, including you!"

Aggravated, he walked away. "You're impossible to talk to, Carol."

He was right; I was impossible to talk to. I calmed myself down and changed my tone.

"Listen, Richard, this healing stuff interests me, I just wanted to check it out, that's all."

Finally, he agreed to take me.

"But I want you to know if it gets weird, I am out of there, do you understand?"

"Yes, of course Richard, and I will be right behind you if it does get weird, you can be sure of that!"

CHAPTER EIGHTEEN

The Battle For My Tortured Soul

The Service Begins

*T*he service was about to begin. Richard came waltzing in and sat down beside me. His eyes were blood red.

"Where have you been?" I asked.

"Never mind, I am here now," he snapped.

Linda showed up and sat on the other side of me.

The musicians came out, picked up their instruments and started playing. The crowd stood to their feet and began singing and clapping.

"I am not singing with these people, this is a circus," Richard muttered. He crossed his arms and remained in his seat.

I stood up, but my body language made it clear I did not want to be a part of this.

Finally, the music stopped—I was relieved. A man stepped up to the platform; he smiled and reached for the microphone.

"That's Pastor Reid," Linda informed me.

"Praise the Lord," the pastor said excitedly.

The crowd went wild, enthusiastically clapping and cheering.

"Oh brother," I murmured.

"Are you glad to be in the House of the Lord?"

Again, they burst into applause.

The pastor proceeded to take an offering. Gold-colored plates were passed up and down the aisles. I peered into the offering plate as it went by. It was laden with checks and cash; I also spotted a gold ring. Someone had actually taken off his or her ring and threw it in!

Richard snickered, "What a racket. I'd like to be the one who counts that stash!"

Then the music started and the people stood up and began singing again. This time, like Richard, I remained seated. A man in an expensive suit came out and joined the pastor on the platform. They chatted briefly; he walked to the podium, reached for the microphone and joined in singing with the people.

After they sang for the longest hour of my life ... the music stopped! The man on the platform stood still as if he was listening for some invisible voice to instruct him.

"That's the speaker," Linda whispered to me. "He's really anointed."

"Anointed? What the heck is that, Linda?"

"Just watch," she replied.

When he opened his tattered Bible and started reading, no one moved; you could hear a pin drop. I looked over at Richard; he shook his head and rolled his eyes. I sighed and leaned back in the seat. Reluctantly, I listened. What else could I do?

The Jesus Factor

"The death of Jesus was horrific," the preacher explained. "First, the soldiers punched him in the face and ripped out his beard with their bare hands. They spit in his face and then beat him with whips, tearing his back to shreds. He was then forced to drag a wooden cross to the top of a hill, where they stripped him naked and nailed him to it. Then he was hoisted up for all to see."

I had heard these things as a kid in church, but never like this. I found myself intrigued with the details.

The preacher continued, "This was the death sentence for criminals, known as crucifixion. The thing is ... this Jesus was innocent! After hours of suffering, he died. His beaten, swollen body was placed in a dark, damp tomb and an enormous boulder was positioned at the entrance, ensuring that no one could get in or out. Three days later, Jesus came out of the grave and showed himself, alive. Over 500 people witnessed this miraculous event."

He ended his message by telling the crowd that the Blood Jesus shed on the cross was the defining factor that saved men and women from an eternal separation from God, which he explained is called "hell."

All righty then! Sounds like a good rap, but is it real? Besides, how can this preacher prove what he's saying is true? Jesus is not here to back him up!

I was convinced the whole thing was a sham—another religious hoax—and I was not buying into it like the rest of these weak, pathetic people!

I'm Outta Here

I stood up. "Linda, we're leaving. I'll see you at work tomorrow."

She grabbed my arm. "Carol, please stay a little longer, the best part of the service is about to take place!"

She looked over at Richard; he nodded in approval, which surprised me. Reluctantly, I sat back down and directed my attention to the man on the platform. He was now inviting people to come and be prayed for. I watched as a stream of people headed up to the front.

I wondered, *How real is this forgiveness and new beginning stuff? How could all the insane things that I have done ever be forgiven and forgotten? And, if heaven is real, then they probably have a special guard at the entrance to keep my butt out!*

Besides, I made a bargain with the devil, and there was no reneging on that deal. The very thought of it sent the "ones within" into a fury. I started to shake physically. Richard looked over at me.

"What is wrong with you?" he asked.

"I feel sick."

"Do you want to leave?"

"Yes!" I answered. I tried to get up, but my legs buckled under me and I fell back on the seat.

"Get out of here!" the "ones within" demanded.

My hands were ice cold, my legs were numb, and my stomach muscles were in spasms. I was a mess!

Beth Joins in the Battle For My Soul

Then I heard an old familiar voice—it was Beth!

"See, Carol, you came to this blasted place and look what is happening to you! You're going crazy again; you belong back in that mental institution!"

My heart was pounding as my eyes darted around the crowded building. Suddenly, the faces of the people started changing; they looked distorted. I felt like they were pointing and laughing at me. I dug my nails into my flesh, gritted my teeth and bit my tongue. I tasted blood.

"Your soul is already owned," the "ones within" reminded me. "You sold it a long time ago. In return, you got us. There is no redemption for you, Carol!"

At that moment, I wanted to crawl under the pew and dissolve.

"Come up and let the Lord heal your body and soul," the preacher cried out.

In my head, I could hear the spirits shouting, "You're a whore and a drug addict, and nobody wants you in this church!"

Richard nudged me. "What the heck is wrong with you? You're having one those moments, aren't you?"

I could feel my head being jerked back, like something had a hold of it.

I was losing it; I had to get out of there—I had to!

Linda Boldly Intervenes

I felt a gentle touch on my arm. I opened my eyes; it was Linda.

She saw the look of torment and fear on my face. "Carol, please let me take you up for prayer."

I stared into her beautiful blue eyes and wondered, *Why does she care?*

She reached over and took my hand. I slowly got up from my seat, and together we walked out to the aisle and down to the front.

As we made our way, Beth and the "ones within" continued to torment me. I felt like daggers were being plunged into my chest. I was dizzy and the room was spinning. The desire to do this was strong, but the war for my soul was making it difficult. I growled; it was not loud but obvious to those standing nearby.

The preacher spotted me in the crowd and instructed the ushers to bring me up on the platform. When they came to get me, Linda released my hand.

"This is where you go it alone, Carol," she said softly. Then she turned and went back to her seat.

I climbed the stairs to the platform. The glare of the house lights stung my eyes.

"Stop the music," the preacher ordered.

Everything got quiet.

I must have been a sight—breasts exposed, yellow skin, red eyes, tight jeans and dirty boots.

The Battle of Good and Evil

"What is the condition of your body?" the preacher asked me.

"I have chronic Hepatitis B," I told him.

"What is that?"

"It's a liver condition. I'm dying."

There was a gasp from the audience.

"Do you believe that Jesus can heal you?"

I refused to answer. In my head, I could hear the words "Jesus is dead!"

The preacher instructed the congregation, "People, pray!"

Three thousand people stood to their feet and started praying. Men, women and children all joined together to pray for a demon-possessed, drug-addicted, dying pagan witch!

Who are these people and why do they care? I wondered.

Then, without warning, I felt a strange power go through me. I crumbled to the floor.

When the usher reached down to help me up, the preacher shouted, "No! Don't touch her! God is doing something here!"

It is difficult to describe what happened to me next, as it was not a physical thing, but spiritual. Pictures of my past went off in my head like a slide show. One by one, they flashed before my eyes, and with each image, I experienced a plethora of emotions: rejection, sorrow, remorse, shame, brokenness, disappointment and betrayal!

I felt like I was a little girl lying there on the carpet, all alone. I was a castaway, unwanted and unloved. I cried out from the depth of my heart, "I want to know where love is!"

An Indescribable Peace

At that moment, I felt the presence of someone standing over me. It was not an usher, nor the speaker; who then? Suddenly, an indescribable feeling of peace began to flow through me. It started at my head and traveled down to my feet. It was amazing!

Then, the kindest voice I'd ever heard said to me, "Carol, my name is Jesus Christ and if you are looking for love, you found it. I love you just the way you are!"

A sob broke out from the center of my being, releasing a flood of tears.

During this whole time, the "ones within" were silent. In the past, my attempts to quiet them were futile, until now!

An usher helped me to my feet and escorted me to the stairs.

As I was walking back to my seat, the preacher called out, "Young lady," and I whirled around to face him. I looked into his fiery eyes, and with a thundering voice, he declared, "You will never be the same!"

When I got back to my seat, Richard didn't utter a word. Linda smiled at me; her blue eyes were pools of tears.

After the service, Richard and I drove home in silence. He pulled in the driveway, parked the car, went up the stairs and fell into the bed. I was not surprised. As for me, I sat up late into the night trying to relive the whole experience. What happened to me at that service was unlike anything I had ever experienced in my life!

CHAPTER NINETEEN

The New Me

Morning Has Broken

After a long night of contemplation and soul searching, I finally slipped off into a drug-free sleep. When I woke, I felt different.

Instead of getting on the phone to my drug supplier, I wanted to call my druggie friends and tell them what had happened to me. However, I refrained; I decided to let this thing play out and see how strong I would be when the urge to get high came knocking at the door. Would I fall back into drugs or walk away?

I sat at the kitchen window, peering down at the street below. The sound of children playing was delightful. The sun pouring in and warming my face felt wonderful. I caught a glimpse of myself in the mirror. I was smiling! Oh happy day, I was smiling!

I decided to surprise Richard with a nice breakfast. When he came out from the bedroom, he had a funny look on his face. I greeted him with a cup of coffee. He sat at the table, ate his eggs, and then mumbled something about having to go out. Ordinarily, I would have argued with him.

225

However, I let him go without any resistance. I was amazed at my new attitude, and to be honest, I think he was too.

About two o'clock in the afternoon, Linda called. She asked me how I was doing. I gave her a lengthy explanation, telling her how happy I was and that I did not even want to get high.

"I know, Carol, this is a supernatural occurrence that has happened to you."

Linda was correct. What happened to me the night before was not just a religious experience or some emotional high; this was something *extra-ordinary*.

The Return of Beth and the "Ones Within"

I knew that Beth and the "ones within" were not intending to give up that easily. When and how they were planning to regain control, I did not know.

One afternoon, about two weeks later, they made a comeback. It happened when I was in the bathroom cleaning up. Suddenly, I couldn't breathe. It felt like someone had thrown a heavy blanket over my head. I called out to Richard.

He came running. "What is the matter, Carol?"

I turned and faced him; he stepped back in horror.

"There is something evil in this room," he whispered.

Then I became nauseated. I bent over the toilet and retched. Richard panicked and took off. I caught my reflection in the mirror; there were dark circles under my eyes, and the vomit was running down my chin into the toilet. I was jerking and shaking.

"Jesus!" I cried in a loud voice. "Help me, please!"

At that moment, the room filled with the same presence

I had felt on the floor of the church. It was calming, yet powerful. I could sense the "ones within" shrieking and squirming. Then in an instant, they were gone. They were forced out by this new power and presence in me, which was far greater than they were. The dark forces to which I had sold my soul no longer had possession of it! I did not understand it all, but I knew it was real, and I was free—free to love, free to live and free to start over again.

My Child Back in My Arms

I had a deep longing to see my daughter, so I called the foster parents and asked them to send her home. When Marilynn walked through the door, my heart skipped a beat. I didn't know how to act. Now I was seeing her through different eyes. This child was a gift given to me—a precious gift—and for so long I had not realized it.

That day, for the first time in years, I held my little girl in my arms; the feeling of her heart beating against my breast was indescribable. I kissed her cheeks, and when she smiled, I melted. We played together in the back yard, and later that afternoon, we took a long walk. As I listened to the sound of her voice telling me about her new friend at school, I realized that I had not listened to a thing she had to say in a very long time, as I was so consumed with drugs and my pitiful life.

"Can I sleep home tonight, Mom?" Marilynn asked as we munched on peanut butter and jelly sandwiches.

"Of course you can, honey," I answered.

That night, we cuddled on the couch and watched a family movie. When Marilynn fell asleep, I carried her to bed and lay down beside her. I wanted to feel my sweet child, smell her and hold her close to me. So many years had gone by and I had missed these most precious moments. I wasn't going to let that happen again because now, I'd been given a second chance to recapture our life together and be a devoted mother.

Yes, Marilynn would visit the family who so graciously took care of her in my absence, but they would only be visits. From now on, my daughter's home would be with me. I had made a promise to her when she was born, that I would love her and protect her. For years, I had failed. Now I intended to keep that promise!

Mountains to Climb, Battles to Fight

As for my marriage, I wish I could say that Richard and I were able to pick up the pieces of our life and go on together, but unfortunately, it didn't turn out that way. Years later, he had an affair with a girl who was much younger than him, and he walked out. Shortly after, he fathered two children with her. I would be lying if I said that it had no effect on me, because it did at the time. However, I was able to extend the same mercy and forgiveness to him that God had so graciously extended to me. In time, I was healed of the pain of his betrayal. Some relationships are like glass; it is better to let them go rather than get hurt by trying to put them back together again.

I also wish I could say that the road from where I was, to where I am today, has been an easy one. On the contrary, I've had some tough mountains to climb and I have scraped and bloodied my knees going over them. Still, Jesus has been there for me through it all.

Am I a Jesus Freak?

Some have mocked me by asking, "Carol, are you a Jesus freak?"

I answer them, "No, I was a freak that Jesus turned into a human being!"

Others see my transformation as being weak, so they ask, "Isn't Jesus a crutch for you?"

My answer: "If He is, I'll take two."

The people that knew me during my years of drugs and crazy living are in awe of the radical change that has taken place in my life.

Others laugh and call me "religious," in the same way that I treated Linda Smith when I first met her. I just smile and tell them, "Hey, whatever anyone may think, the change in me cannot be denied, disputed, argued or explained in natural terms. It was not pills, an institution, counseling sessions, or a rehabilitation facility that changed my life. No, it was a divine appointment for me to meet The Great Healer."

Never the Same

For all those years, I had blamed God for everything that went wrong in my life. Now I realize I was mistaken because He loved me and was watching over me, even when I was unaware of it and in complete rebellion. I had sold my soul to an evil force, as I was deceived into believing it was the ultimate power. Consequently, I paid a high price for low living—up until that night on the floor of the church, when a supernatural power reached down into the gutter, to where I lay dying, and pulled me out. Christ paid the utmost price through his death and was the only one who had the power

to redeem my soul. He looked past all of my faults and fail-
ures and found some value and worth in my brutally damaged, broken soul. He bought it back and gave me a new life,
and since that day, *I have never been the same!*

Epilogue

Then What Happened?

My dear reader,

Many people have come to me, after they have heard my story, with a variety of questions. You may have some yourself. Therefore, I have listed the most frequently asked and added my answers. I hope you find "your" question among them.

Question: What are you doing now, Carol?

Answer: I have been traveling internationally for the last twenty years, telling my story. I speak on various subjects and I am a Bible teacher. I have appeared on radio and television. I speak at conferences, seminars and churches around the country. I also speak at rehabilitation centers, jails and girls' homes. In addition, I am an author.

Question: Where is your daughter Marilynn now?

Answer: Marilynn has been an integral part of my work for over fifteen years. She is married to a wonderful and talented man (Matthew Bonner), and I have two incredible grandbabies: Aaron and Abigail; they call me "MeMe"!

Question: Do you have any other children?

Answer: No, Marilynn is my only child.

Question: What happened to your father?

Answer: He escaped from the mental hospital and fled to

North Carolina, where he lived with his brother, Victor. One morning he complained of a headache and retired to his room. He went into a coma and later died of an aneurysm. He was a lonely, broken man. The last time I talked to him was on the phone at Christmastime. He was crying and wanted to come home. The hospital would have committed him, so Mom warned him to stay away. That day he talked to each one of his children. When I got on the phone, he told me that he loved me and missed me. Years after his death, I found out that he is indeed my biological father. My dad suffered with physical illness and depression. The things he did were not his fault, but a result of his illness. I truly believe he loved me, and I can say from my heart: I love him too!

Question: Did you and your mother (Dorothy) ever reconcile?

Answer: This is the best part of the whole story. After I changed, my mother had a spiritual experience and she too had a "miraculous" transformation. I was skeptical at first and I harbored bitter feelings for her. However, God granted me the grace to listen to her side of the story and to forgive her. Then, I humbly asked her to forgive me. When my mother took me in her arms for the first time and I laid my head upon her warm breast, I wept for joy. All those years, I had longed for that moment and God gave it to me! Dorothy died at 78 years old. Before she went to heaven, she let each of her children know how much she loved them. Every year on my birthday, she sent a card with a message expressing how proud of me she was and that she loved me. I am honored to say that I am Dorothy's daughter. (In my book *Betrayal, the Deepest Cut,* I cover the whole encounter of our reconciliation.)

Question: Do you see Richard anymore?

Answer: Not much, he has his life and I have mine. I truly wish him the best.

Question: What about Louie, Marilynn's father?

Answer: When I met and married Richard, Louie and I parted ways. Years later, Louie died of brain tumors. Marilynn (his only child) and I visited him at the hospital. They held on to each other for a long time. I was there the night before he died. Louie could not talk, *but his eyes told the story.*

Question: Are you ever tempted to use drugs again?

Answer: To be perfectly honest, no. There is "no high, like the most High!" That being Jesus Christ. Why go back? What is there to go back to? Death? I am free ... free indeed!

Question: What happened to Sarah, your roommate? Is she still practicing witchcraft?

Answer: Not that I know of. She is now married and has children.

Question: Do you still see Linda Smith?

Answer: Great question! I see Linda when I am in the Buffalo area. She still works as a disc jockey for weddings and special events. Linda continues to reach out to those who are the "castaways." I have never met anyone quite like her; she is truly a rare jewel!

Question: Have the "ones within" or Beth made any reappearances?

Answer: They would not dare! Greater is He that is in me!

Question: Having been sick for so long, how is your health now?

Answer: The Hepatitis B is no longer detectable in my body. The ulcers are gone and I feel wonderful! It has been over twenty years and I'm still kickin'!

Question: How old are you now?

Answer: Ah, age is a number and mine is unlisted!

In Conclusion

My precious reader,

*I pray my story has given you **hope**. Remember, don't ever give up and don't believe that God cannot reach the unreachable, because He can and He will! I am living proof that HE IS ABLE!*

For more books and materials by Carol Kornacki,
please visit www.carolkornacki.org.